French Provincial Cookery

DAVID & CHARLES

Newton Abbot London

British Library Cataloguing in Publication Data
French provincial cookery.—(David & Charles Kitchen Workshop)
  1. Cookery, French.
  I. Fransk bondekost.   *English*
  641.5944   TX719

  ISBN 0-7153-8477-5

© Text: David & Charles 1983
  Colour illustrations: A/S Hjemmet 1980
  Line illustrations: A/S Hjemmet 1980

Filmset by MS Filmsetting Limited, Frome, Somerset
and printed in The Netherlands
by Smeets Offset BV, Weert
for David & Charles (Publishers) Limited,
Brunel House, Newton Abbot, Devon

Introduction

It is not quite correct to use the expression 'art of cooking' in connection with French provincial cuisine – it is part of the French way of life. They don't overload their food with elaborate trimmings or superfluous decoration – good, simple raw materials are turned into tasty dishes suited to the particular season, the climate, and the type of work the people are involved in.

It is quite natural that they should make substantial meat dishes with cabbage and other more solid vegetables in the north, whereas in the south they make colourful vegetable dishes with just a little meat. The food is simply adjusted to the daily life and whatever the farm, kitchen garden or local market has to offer.

A French housewife uses the raw materials available in the near vicinity and uses them when they are at their best. She serves butter-steamed peas with small fresh onions and lettuce when she has these vegetables in her larder or when they are especially cheap in the food market.

A hen's days are numbered if, come autumn, she does not lay any more eggs. She will go into the pot, along with fresh vegetables in season. This fits in with the sense of economy a French housewife is born with. She does not buy frozen beans in February when they can be picked in the garden, or bought fresh and a lot cheaper, in the fruit market in July.

In a French farm kitchen everything is used – very rarely is something edible thrown out. If the onions are sprouting, the green sprouts are finely chopped and used in soups and casseroles. They add a nice touch of colour and flavour, without costing anything. The fat from roast meat or poultry is used in a sauce, or simply as fat for frying. You get a nice flavour for nothing.

French Districts and Their Specialities

It is impossible here to go into great detail, for every province and village has its own speciality, characteristic

4

of that particular place. But this brief summary will be enough to underline the logical connection between scenery and gastronomy.

Languedoc – Provence

These two Mediterranean districts, situated on either side of the Rhône, illustrate everything we mean when we speak of cooking from the South of France.

Here they use olive oil instead of butter, garlic, olives and sunripened tomatoes, shiny deep-purple aubergines and fresh herbs and spices from sundrenched mountainsides. There are omelettes filled with peppers, extremely spicy garlic sausages, roast mutton with herbs and spices, small, strong-flavoured cheeses wrapped in vine leaves, peaches, fresh figs, melons and cherries. And to go with all this there is the local wine – heavy red wine from Languedoc and rosé from Provence. There are dishes from these districts on pages 11, 17, 21, 33, 49 and 51.

Bordeaux – Gascony

In the south-west corner of France there is the lowland along the Bay of Biscay and the mountainous area bordering on Spain. The cooking here is influenced in the north by the important wine district, and in the south by Spanish tradition.

Along the coast there are vast quantities of fish and shellfish and these, of course, feature in the cuisine. Poultry is a popular ingredient both in the north and south. As in the Strasbourg area, several delicacies are made from geese. Goose Liver Mousse, for instance, is served on festive occasions, spread on slices of brown bread, as an hors d'oeuvre.

Many housewives still keep a large earthenware jug, containing cooked goose meat covered with melted goose fat, in their larder.

In the Basque area, substantial dishes made from beef and pork predominate. They also make lovely, spicy sausages which they fry in either lard or butter and oil.

Loire – Burgundy

It is the river and its fertile valley sides, covered with vines, which influence the food in the Loire district. Here we find freshwater fish, delicately prepared and served with a glass of the local white wine, fresh vegetables in abundance, butter and cheese and, of course, grapes.

Further to the east is Burgundy, a quite different wine district, with heady red wines. As in the Loire valley, the wine decides the food – dishes like Coq au Vin (page 40) and Boeuf à la Moutarde de Dijon (page 37).

Dijon mustard, which originates from this area, adds flavour to the meat, fish, poultry, game and sausages.

Alsace – Lorraine

The cooking in the districts along France's eastern border is heavily influenced by neighbouring Germany. The food here is filling – thick soups and filling meat dishes with cabbage and root vegetables, often boiled with spicy sausages bought from the village butcher.

The famous and expensive Strasbourg Goose Liver Pâté originates from this district, but the main fare is roasts and sausages with a number of variations of pâtés and meat in aspic. The Munster cheese

originates from here, having been invented by monks as far back as the seventh century – hence the name which is a derivation from the word *monastère* (monastery). With this the locals drink their white Alsace wine. And we must not forget the famous tart with cheese, cream and eggs – Quiche Lorraine (see page 59).

Another dish from this district, not quite so well known, is the filling and tasty Potée Lorraine (see page 29).

Normandy, Picardy, Ile de France

The districts in the north – Picardy, Ile de France and Normandy – are agricultural districts, ideal for dairy farming. From these areas come the best butter, the thickest cream and the very best cheeses – Camembert for instance.

The countryside around Rouen is well known for fat, tasty ducks, and the large apple farms found everywhere in Normandy produce cider and the apple liqueur Calvados.

On the coast there is everything you could wish for in the range of fish and shellfish, and the lambs grazing here – on the shores of the English Channel – have an unusual and delicate salty flavour.

Typical recipes from these areas are to be found on pages 14, 22, 24, 47 and 63.

Lyons – Rhône

South of Burgundy is the Rhône district. The cooking is influenced by the heady local wines and here you will find poultry, pâtés and hams. The cervelat sausage originates from this district.

More pork is used here and there are various special dishes made from whole and minced fish. There are also several dishes consisting of pot-roasted meat and fresh vegetables, which go very well with the local wine, Beaujolais. On page 16 there is a recipe for a soup characteristic of this area.

Brittany

A great part of this district consists of coastal cliffs, and the soil is meagre. The main ingredient in the local dishes is fish and, above all, shellfish. But here again we find salty lamb meat, excellent poultry and vegetables.

Here, too, they grow the large, heavy artichokes which are strong enough to withstand long transport, and are therefore sold in most parts of Europe.

Recipes from Brittany are on pages 20 and 44.

The Recipes and Their Ingredients

You can buy all the ingredients for the various dishes in this book in this country, and the majority of the recipes are surprisingly inexpensive to make.

You will find a relatively large number of soup recipes. The French housewife serves soup at both lunch and dinner, which may inspire us to make soup more often. There are many tasty and economical recipes to choose from.

Dishes made from stewed and pot-roasted meat are well represented because they are common in France, and because they show clearly how clever the French housewife is when it comes to making cheap cuts go a long way.

Possibly there is more concentration than usual on vegetables. But vegetables are a very important part of a French meal. A vegetable dish is always prepared with care and consists of the very best raw materials. If you have difficulty in getting hold of fresh vegetables, frozen ones are the best alternative. Only rarely is the canned variety a good substitute, apart from canned tomatoes which have good flavour and are reasonable in price. Aubergines, artichokes and other vegetables which are not cultivated to a great extent in this country, are imported and widely available on the supermarket shelves. Always keep an eye on vegetable prices. Imported ones can be surprisingly inexpensive, especially when they are in season in their country of origin.

To avoid confusion, it should be noted that, unless stated otherwise, the fennel used in the recipes is not herb fennel but the imported Florentine fennel. It is usually available in supermarkets, looking like celery but more bulbous at the base. It can be used raw in salads, or

cooked, and tastes of aniseed.

In the recipes containing cheese, Gruyère – a cheese not unlike Emmenthaler – is mostly used. Although the result may not be quite so authentic, it can successfully be replaced by a good-flavoured Cheddar.

The more typical French dessert cheeses, often served there before fresh fruit or other dessert, are imported in a varied selection.

There are very few dessert recipes in the book. This is because the dessert does not play a very important part in an everyday French dinner, which frequently consists of soup or a starter followed by fish and/or meat, salad and/or a hot vegetable dish – rather a lot already. It is understandable that the French housewife rounds off a meal with fresh fruit instead of dessert. But for the Sunday family dinner they make a special effort, just as we do. The meal is then usually rounded off with a fruit tart, a soufflé or pancakes.

Traditional Soups

French soups have a reputation well beyond the boundaries of France, and rightly too! The economical French housewife leaves a pot of soup simmering on the cooker practically twenty-four hours a day.

Every now and then she makes a good, filling meat stock, to be served with the meat on the first day and as a soup with plenty of vegetables added, or in gravies, stews and casseroles in the days ahead.

The French even have a proverb dedicated to soups: 'If you want to save money, eat soup for dinner.' Or, in French: 'Pour faire des économies, il faut manger le potage.'

Pot au Feu

Pot au feu – which means the pot on the fire – is the most usual stock. It is made of beef, usually from comparatively cheap cuts from the brisket or shin. These cuts have the right mixture of meat and fat to give the stock a rich flavour. You can also add a beef marrow bone. Boiled marrow served on brown bread with sea salt is a delicacy. A veal knuckle gives the stock an even richer flavour.

Good meat stock is the basis for many tasty soups. Here mushrooms, tomatoes, green vegetables and rice have been added.

Clear Meat Stock – Pot au Feu

(makes 4–5 litres [7–9pt])
Preparation time: 30–40 min
Cooking time: about 3 hr
Strained stock is suitable for the freezer

2kg (4½lb) shin of beef
1–2 marrow bones
3–4 veal bones
salt, 2 onions
5 carrots
2 stalks of celery
4–5 leeks
12 whole black peppercorns
2 bay leaves
1 sprig of thyme
3–4 stems of parsley

1 Dry meat with a damp cloth.
2 Wrap the marrow bones in gauze to prevent the marrow from escaping when boiling. Place all the bones in a saucepan large enough to hold at least 6–7 litres (10½–12pt). Place the meat on top of the bones and add 4–5 litres (7–9pt) cold water. Bring slowly to the boil and skim carefully several times.
3 Clean and scrape carrots, clean leeks. Whole onions with no blemishes need only thorough rinsing – the brown skin adds a nice golden colour to the stock. Make a bouquet garni using the green part of the leeks, a few celery leaves, bay leaves, thyme, parsley and peppercorns.
4 Place vegetables and bouquet garni in the saucepan, add 3 × 5ml tsp (3tsp) salt, and cover. Lower the heat, so that the contents are just boiling. When meat and bones have simmered for about 1 hr, remove the marrow bones and the bouquet garni. If you wish to serve the marrow warm, put the bones back into the pot when 1 hr remains of cooking time.
5 Take meat out of the saucepan and keep it warm in a casserole with a lid on, or place it in a smaller saucepan with some of the stock. Remove bones and vegetables with a slotted spoon. Pick any meat off the bones and place this with the meat. There is no taste or goodness in the vegetables after such a long boiling – if you wish to serve vegetables with the meat and soup, boil fresh ones.
6 Strain the stock through a sieve.

Ladle out the stock you need now, bring to the boil with salt to taste and add a few thin leek rings, finely chopped parsley or several kinds of freshly boiled vegetables. The soup can also be served as a clear consommé, with a raw egg yolk in each plate.
7 Allow the remaining stock to boil, covered, for a short time, how long depends on what consistency you want. Cool stock and remove some of the fat which has come to the top. This fat has a lot of flavour and is therefore excellent for frying in general or when preparing sauces and stews.
8 Deep freeze the stock in convenient portions. Use strong freezing bags or cartons. It will keep for 3–4 months at a temperature of not more than −18°C, 0°F. Strain stock after defrosting.
9 The meat can be served with vegetables and a sauce – caper, mushroom, sweet and sour sauce – or horseradish cream.

Clear Mushroom Soup – Potage aux Champignons

(serves 4)
Preparation time: 15–20 min
Cooking time: about 15 min
Unsuitable for the freezer

1 onion, 50g (2oz) butter
1 stalk of celery OR
1 slice of celeriac
1–2 cloves garlic (optional)
350–450g (¾–1lb) mushrooms
1–1½ litres (1¾–2½pt) Clear Meat Stock
3–4 tomatoes, 2 cups of boiled long-grain rice
a few lettuce leaves
salt and pepper

1 Coarsely chop the onion and steam in the butter in a saucepan for about 5 min on low heat. Add finely chopped celery or coarsely grated celeriac and crushed garlic.
2 Rinse mushrooms, slice and put in the saucepan. Fry gently for 3–4 min and sprinkle with a little salt.
3 Scald and skin tomatoes, quarter and add to saucepan. Add stock, boiled rice and finely shredded lettuce. Boil for 6–8 min on low heat. Season with salt and pepper.
Serve hot with brown bread or croissants.

White Cabbage Soup – Potage au Chou

(serves 4)
Preparation time: 15–20 min
Cooking time: about 20 min
Suitable for the freezer, but will lose some flavour

200–300g (7–11oz) white cabbage
2 stalks of celery
2 shallots
2 leeks
1 clove garlic (optional)
2–3 × 15ml tbsp (2–3tbsp) olive oil
1–1½ litres (1¾–2½pt) meat stock
1 bay leaf
1 sprig of thyme
½ × 5ml tsp (½tsp) mixed herbs
40g (1½oz) macaroni
salt, pepper
parsley

1 Clean all vegetables and cut into thin strips. Crush or finely chop garlic.
2 Sauté vegetables lightly in the oil. Add stock and macaroni and boil for about 10 min. Add seasoning and herbs to taste, and boil until everything is tender but not mushy.
3 Sprinkle with chopped parsley. Serve with brown rolls.

Onion Soup – Soupe à l'Oignon

(serves 4)
Preparation time: 15–20 min
Cooking time: 20–25 min
Suitable for the freezer without toasted cheese bread

5 large onions
oil, butter
1–1½ litres (1¾–2¼pt) stock
1 bay leaf
salt, pepper
150ml (¼pt) dry white wine
½ French loaf
grated cheese

Left: White Cabbage Soup with brown rolls.

1 Peel onions, slice into thin rings and sauté in 1 × 15ml tbsp (1tbsp) oil and 1 × 15ml tbsp (1tbsp) butter until golden. Add stock, bay leaf, salt and pepper and simmer on low heat until onion is tender. Stir in white wine.

2 Slice and toast bread. Lightly butter the toast, sprinkle a thick layer of grated cheese on top and brown under the grill.

3 Pour soup into individual dishes, or into one large one. Put slices of cheese bread on each serving.

Vegetable Soup – Soupe au Pistou
(serves 4)
Preparation time: 15–20 min
Cooking time: about 20 min
Suitable for the freezer, but will lose some flavour

1 onion
3 carrots
3 potatoes
1 stalk of celery
2 leeks
200g (7oz) green beans
salt and pepper
1 × 15ml tbsp (1tbsp) butter or oil
1½ litres (2½pt) meat stock
75g (3oz) noodles or ribbon spaghetti
1 clove garlic
1 large tomato
2 × 15ml tbsp (2tbsp) fresh or
*   1 × 5ml tsp (1tsp) dried basil*

1 Clean and slice vegetables. Sauté in butter or oil and sprinkle with salt and pepper. Add stock and boil for 10 mins on low heat.

Above: Vegetable Soup has noodles or spaghetti as one of the ingredients.

2 Add noodles or spaghetti to soup and boil until just tender.

3 Scald and skin tomato. Crush with the garlic and basil. Stir in a couple of spoonsful of hot soup and add back to the soup. Adjust seasoning, if necessary.

Serve with grated cheese and bread rolls.

Onion Soup with toasted cheese is delicious.

11

This large photograph shows a selection of the delicious fresh vegetables a French housewife can choose from. In the soup dish is a thickened meat soup with new potatoes, shallots, carrots, green beans and peas.
Fish Soup (above) is full of tasty vegetables.

Fish Soup – Soupe de Poissons
(serves 4)
Preparation time: 15 min
Cooking time: 25–30 min
Unsuitable for the freezer

$\frac{1}{2}kg$ *(1lb 2oz) cleaned firm fish (eg lumpfish or halibut)*
2 carrots, 2 leeks
1 stalk of celery
salt, pepper
1 small parsnip (optional)
4–5 potatoes
1 bay leaf, 1 sprig of parsley

1 Slice cleaned and skinned fish. Sprinkle with a little salt.
2 Clean the vegetables, slice and bring to the boil for 20 min in 1–1¼ litres (1¾–2¼pt) water, adding 1 × 5ml tsp (1tsp) salt, ¼ × 5ml tsp (¼tsp) pepper and a bouquet garni of leek top, bay leaf and ½ sprig of parsley.
3 Remove bouquet garni, place fish slices in saucepan, bring to the boil again, and skim well. Boil on low heat until fish is cooked. Season again, and serve hot with brown bread.

Thick soups

In France, thick soups are often a mixture of mashed vegetables and vegetables kept whole. As a rule a blend of milk, cream or crème fraîche (the thick, slightly soured cream which can be used instead of sour cream), is added as a final touch.

**Potato Soup with Cheese –
Potage Crème de Pommes de terres
et du Fromage** (left)
(serves 5–6)
Preparation time: 15 min
Cooking time: about 30 min
Unsuitable for the freezer

½kg (1lb 2oz) potatoes
2 onions
1 clove garlic
4 leeks
15–25g (½–1oz) butter
salt, pepper
turmeric, nutmeg
1½–2 litres (2½–3½pt) Clear Meat
    Stock (see page 9)
250ml (9fl oz) cream
about 200g (7oz) cheese (Swiss or
    Cheddar)

1 Clean and slice vegetables. Crush or finely chop garlic. Steam both in butter on low heat for 6–8 min. Add salt, pepper, ¼–½ × 5ml tsp (¼–½tsp) turmeric and meat stock.
2 Boil, covered, until vegetables are tender, then remove half of them with a slotted spoon. Allow remainder to boil until quite soft and rub through a fine sieve or purée in a blender.
3 Place vegetables back into soup,

bring to the boil and stir in warm cream, about 100g (¼lb) grated cheese and a little grated nutmeg. Stir until cheese has melted, but do not allow soup to boil. Serve hot with a couple of slices of cheese.

**Chive Soup –
Potage à la Ciboulette** (centre)
(serves 4)
Preparation time: 10 min
Cooking time: 20–25 min
Unsuitable for the freezer

2 shallots
2–3 leeks
½kg (1lb 2oz) potatoes
15g (½oz) butter
¾ litre (about 1¼pt) Clear Meat
    Stock (see page 9)
½ litre (1pt) milk
salt, pepper
2 handfuls of chives
150ml (¼pt) dry white wine
    (optional)

1 Clean vegetables and cut into small pieces, using only the light part of the leeks.

2 Sauté vegetables in the butter on strong heat, add stock and boil until vegetables are completely tender. Rub through a fine sieve or purée in a blender.

3 Heat soup with the boiling milk. Add salt, pepper and finely chopped chives. Season with white wine if wished. Serve soup hot with a crisp French loaf or wholewheat bread.

VARIATIONS

Potato Soup with Watercress – Potage de Pommes de terre au Cresson
Add plenty of finely chopped watercress instead of chives, and replace milk with cream.

Chilled Potato and Leek Soup – Crème Vichyssoise
Follow directions for Chive Soup to end of method 2. Season soup with salt and pepper and chill. Stir 100–200ml (4–7fl oz) whipped cream into soup and serve ice-cold. Put an ice cube and a sprinkling of chopped chives into each bowl.

Farmhouse Soup – Potage à la Bonne Femme (right)
(serves 4)
Preparation time 10–15 min
Cooking time: about 30 min
Unsuitable for the freezer

225g (½lb) bacon
2 onions
½kg (1lb 2oz) potatoes
4 carrots
4 leeks
1 stalk of celery
1 × 15ml tbsp (1tbsp) butter or oil
1–1½ litres (1¼–2½pt) stock
100–200ml (4–7fl oz) double cream
salt, pepper

3–4 sprigs of parsley
1 sprig of thyme
celery leaves
chopped parsley to garnish

1 Cut bacon into strips and sauté until golden in a heavy casserole. Remove, and pour off the fat.

2 Clean vegetables and cut into small pieces. Add butter or oil to the casserole and put in the vegetables. Simmer on low heat for a few min, add salt and pepper and pour stock over. Make a bouquet garni of leek green, thyme, celery leaves and parsley and place in casserole. Boil vegetables until tender, then remove bouquet garni.

3 Rub vegetables and stock through a fine-meshed sieve or purée in a blender. Bring soup to the boil, stir in warm cream and adjust seasoning. Sprinkle with finely chopped parsley and bacon. Serve soup hot with brown bread.

Soup Casseroles

'Pot au Feu' – Clear Meat Stock (page 9) – is renowned as a tasty bouillon, rather than for its meat content. In these recipes, however, the meat or fish is the most important ingredient.

**Pork Soup with Sausage –
La Soupe au Lard**
(serves 6–8)
Preparation time: 1 hr
Cooking time: about 1½ hr
Strained soup, vegetables and meat are suitable for the freezer, separately

1½kg (3lb) meaty rib of pork
   (without rind but with a thick
   layer of fat)
½kg (1lb 2oz) smoked sausage

1kg (2¼lb) carrots
4 leeks, 1 onion
3 cloves
2 stalks of celery OR 1 slice celeriac
1 green pepper
1 bay leaf
1 sprig of thyme
3–4 sprigs of parsley
salt, pepper
Brine :
2 litres (3½pt) water
300g (11oz) salt
100g (¼lb) sugar

Fish Soup from Provence – Soupe de Poissons Provençale

(serves 4–5)
Preparation time: 30 min
Cooking time: about 50 min
Unsuitable for the freezer

¾kg (1lb 10oz) firm fish on the bone
parsley, 1 bay leaf
¼ × 5ml tsp (¼tsp) dried, or pinch of
* fresh, herb fennel*
salt, peppercorns
olive oil
1 lemon
4 shallots
1 clove garlic
saffron or turmeric
3 tomatoes
½kg (1lb 2oz) boiled mussels
shrimps or shrimp tails

1 Clean fish, remove bones, and boil any head, bones and the like in 1 litre (1¾pt) water with 1–2 × 5ml tsp (1–2tsp) salt, 10 peppercorns, sliced lemon, a few sprigs of parsley, fennel and bay leaf. Boil for at least ½ hr, then strain.

2 Lightly sauté coarsely chopped shallots and crushed garlic in a saucepan containing 1–2 × 15ml tbsp (1–2tbsp) oil, and add a pinch of saffron or ½ × 5ml tsp (½tsp) turmeric, peeled and sliced tomatoes and fish stock. Boil for about 10 min.

3 Rub fish pieces with salt, cut into strips and place in stock. Simmer on low heat until fish is white and firm. Heat shelled shrimps in the soup, but do not allow to boil. Adjust seasoning. Serve with French bread.

1 Bring ingredients for brine to the boil, add pork and simmer for 20 min. Remove and place in a saucepan with 2½ litres (4½pt) cold water. (The pork can be salted the day before, boiled for 15 min in the salt brine and left to cool.)

2 Peel or wash vegetables and slice. Make a bouquet garni of a leek top, celery green, bay leaf, thyme, cloves and parsley. Add a pinch of salt and ¼–½ × 5ml tsp (¼–½tsp) pepper.

3 Remove vegetables as they be-come tender and boil the pork until completely tender. Keep vegetables warm in some of the stock. Season with salt, if necessary.

4 Brown sausage in a little fat or warm it in a colander over the sauce-pan. It should not be allowed to simmer in the stock as this will en-hance the smoky flavour. Serve pork, sausage and warm vegetables on flat, heated plates and soup plates containing soup at the side. Put out brown bread.

Above left: Pork Soup with Sausage.

Above: Fish Soup from Provence – a regional speciality.

Above: Split Peas with Salted Pork.

Meat Soups

These soups are rather time-consuming to make, but the result is well worth waiting for! Each is a meal in its own right, and just the thing on a cold winter's day.

Split Peas with Salted Pork – La soupe aux Pois Chiches
(serves 6–8)
Preparation time: 20 min
Cooking time: about 2 hr
Cooking peas: 30–40 min

1–1½kg (2¼–3lb) lightly salted ridge
   of shoulder of pork
½kg (1lb 2oz) pork sausages
300g (11oz) shallots
6 carrots
1 parsnip
1 small head of celery
4 leeks
½kg (1lb 2oz) split peas
thyme, parsley, celery green
salt and pepper

1 Bring meat and sausages to the boil in water to barely cover. Skim well and add a bouquet garni of leek tops, a couple of sprigs of thyme and parsley and celery green. Remove sausages after about 15 min, but boil meat for a further 1½ hr.
2 Add prepared and sliced vegetables (except peas), remove bouquet garni, and boil until meat and vegetables are tender.
3 Meanwhile boil peas (split peas do not need steeping) in ½ litre (about 1pt) boiling water, adding some of the meat stock after about 15 min. After another 15 min add the remaining stock along with the vegetables. Warm the sausages.
Season soup with salt and pepper and add a little crushed thyme.

Boiling Fowl with Salted Brisket – La Poule au Pot
(left)
(serves 6–8)
Preparation time: 30 min
Cooking time: 2–2½ hr

1kg (2¼lb) lightly salted brisket
½kg (1lb 2oz) lightly salted pork
1 boiling fowl
6 peppercorns
½ head of celery, 8 carrots

6 leeks, 8 shallots
2 bay leaves, parsley
8 small beetroots

1 Place beef and pork in a saucepan containing about 2 litres (3½pt) cold water and bring slowly to the boil. Remove all scum. Place peppercorns, bay leaves and a bouquet garni made from celery green and leek tops in the saucepan, and boil for about 1 hr.

2 Place cooking fowl in saucepan, skim, and boil for ½ hr. Add whole prepared carrots, shallots and leeks, and simmer, covered, until everything is tender.

3 Place washed beetroots in plenty of cold water with 1 × 15ml tbsp (1tbsp) salt. Boil for 30 min, then rinse in cold water and rub off the skins.

4 Arrange meat and vegetables on hot serving dishes. Strain stock, skim off fat and sprinkle with a little finely chopped parsley – sprinkle both meat and vegetables, too, if you wish. Serve the stock as a soup and make a light sauce with grated horseradish for the meat and vegetables.

Lamb Shoulder with Vegetables – Bouilli d'Agneau (above)
(serves 6–8)
Preparation time: 20 min
Cooking time: about 1½ hr

2½kg (5½lb) lamb shoulder or scrag
parsley, 1 sprig of thyme
1 sprig of marjoram or basil
2 onions, 2 cloves garlic
salt, 4 carrots
1 head of celery
½ white cabbage
1 red pepper
200ml (7fl oz) sour cream

1 Place meat in about 2 litres (3½pt) cold water in a saucepan, bring to the boil and skim well. Add sliced onion, finely chopped garlic, 2 × 5ml tsp (2tsp) salt and a bouquet garni of 3 sprigs of parsley, thyme and marjoram or basil. Boil for about 45 min. Remove bouquet garni.

2 Slice remaining vegetables, add to saucepan and boil on low heat until everything is tender. Season with more salt. Arrange meat in slices on a hot serving dish. Pour gravy and vegetables into a tureen and arrange dollops of sour cream on top.

½kg (1lb 2oz) sorrel (or nettles or spinach)
½kg (1lb 2oz) fillets of cod, pollack, pike or other firm fish
salt
butter
1 lemon
1 sliced onion
6–8 peppercorns
chopped fresh tarragon
200ml (7fl oz) cream or sour cream

1 Rinse the sorrel in cold water several times, shake dry.
2 Rub fish with salt and place in a saucepan with 1 × 15ml tbsp (1tbsp) melted butter. Squeeze lemon juice over and add a very little water, the onion and peppercorns. Leave on low heat until cooked.
3 Sauté the sorrel or other leaves in 1 × 15ml tbsp (1tbsp) melted butter until they begin to soften. Add 2 × 15ml tbsp (2tbsp) cooking liquor from the fish, the cream and salt to taste. Boil for a couple of minutes and add a little tarragon. Place on a hot serving dish.
4 Pour fish stock over the green base if you want it moister. Place fish slices on top.
Serve with a crisp French loaf.

Garlic Mayonnaise (Aïoli)
Crush 2 cloves garlic in a bowl and stir in 2 egg yolks. Add 150–200ml (5–7fl oz) olive oil, drop by drop to start with and then in a thin trickle. Flavour with salt and wine vinegar.

Fish Dishes

Along the coasts and rivers of France they serve the most delicious fresh fish dishes, with vegetables in season and other simple but tasty ingredients. Here are a few examples.

**Fish with Sorrel –
Poisson à l'Oseille** (above)
(serves 4)
Preparation time: 30 min
Cooking time: 15–20 min
Unsuitable for the freezer

Cod with Olives –
Morue aux Olives (left)

(serves 4)
Preparation time: 15 min
Marinating time: 45–60 min
Cooking time: 6–10 min
Unsuitable for the freezer

½kg (1lb 2oz) cod fillets
3–4 × 15ml tbsp (3–4tbsp) olive oil
1 clove garlic
salt, pepper
marjoram or tarragon
50–100g (2–4oz) green olives
Marinade: 2 large lemons
2–3 bay leaves

1 Cut fish fillets into pieces and place in marinade.
2 Put olive oil in a large, shallow saucepan and add crushed garlic, 1 × 5ml tsp (1tsp) salt and ¼ × 5ml tsp (¼tsp) coarsely ground pepper.

Place fish and marinade in saucepan and steam on low heat for 6–10 min until fish is cooked.
3 Sprinkle with a little marjoram or tarragon and add olives.

Garlic Fish from Provence –
La Bourride (above)

(serves 5–6)
Preparation time: 45 min
Cooking time: 10–20 min
Unsuitable for the freezer

¾kg (1lb 10oz) cod fillets or dried
*   cod*
1 onion
1 bay leaf
1 lemon
parsley or fennel top
1 × 15ml tbsp (1tbsp) wine vinegar
½ × 5ml tsp (¼tsp) peppercorns
1 × 5ml tsp (1tsp) salt
1 French loaf

2 egg yolks
Garlic Mayonnaise, see page 20

1 Make Garlic Mayonnaise.
2 In a saucepan, boil 1–1½ litres (1¼–2½pt) water with sliced onion, bay leaf, sliced lemon, parsley or fennel, wine vinegar, peppercorns and salt (omit for the dried cod).
3 Place fish in saucepan and cook very gently.
4 Meanwhile toast thin slices of French loaf. Place bowl of garlic mayonnaise in a saucepan of hot water. Add whisked egg yolks and whip in 100–200ml (4–7fl oz) strained fish stock, a little at a time. Whisk until sauce is fluffy but do not, on any account, boil.
5 Place French bread with well-drained fish in a hot dish. Pour sauce over and sprinkle with toasted breadcrumbs.

Fish Stew from Alsace – Matelote Alsacienne (right)

(serves 6–8)
Preparation time: 1 hr
Cooking time: about 1 hr
Unsuitable for the freezer

2kg (4½lb) whole fish (pike, eel, trout etc)
salt, peppercorns
1 onion
1 clove garlic
1 bay leaf, 1 sprig of thyme
3 sprigs of parsley
25g (1oz) butter
250g (9oz) mushrooms
200g (7oz) pearl onions
300ml (½pt) white wine
250ml (9fl oz) double cream
100ml (4fl oz) sour cream
2 egg yolks
asparagus and shrimps for garnish

1 Bone the fish and boil bones, heads etc in 400ml (¾pt) water with 1 × 5ml tsp (1tsp) salt, 12 peppercorns, onion, garlic, bay leaf, thyme and parsley for about 30 min. Strain and allow to boil for a short time uncovered.
2 Add 200ml (7fl oz) wine and slices of lightly salted eel. Simmer for 5 min, then add fish fillets and continue to simmer on very low heat for about 10 min. Remove fish and keep warm in some of the stock. Use a little more stock to warm asparagus and peeled shrimps. Strain remaining stock.
3 Sauté peeled pearl onions in 15g (½oz) butter on low heat for 5 min. Add whole, cleaned mushrooms, salt and a little stock and simmer for 2–3 min.
4 Bring remaining stock to the boil with 100ml (4fl oz) double cream. Whisk egg yolks until fluffy with remaining double cream and stir in. Do not allow to boil. Add sour cream, remaining white wine, salt and remaining butter. Arrange fish, onion and mushrooms in a hot dish, pour sauce over and garnish.

Fish Ragout with Shrimps – Ragoût de Poissons Normand (below)

(serves 4)
Preparation time: 30 min
Cooking time: about 1 hr
Unsuitable for the freezer

1kg (2¼lb) cod, pollock, mackerel or plaice
salt, peppercorns
3 onions
3 sprigs of parsley
1 bay leaf
1 sprig of thyme, herb fennel
2 leeks
2 × 15ml tbsp (2tbsp) oil
2 tomatoes
200ml (7fl oz) white wine
200g (7oz) shrimps
dill

1 Fillet the fish and put heads, bones etc in about 300ml (½pt) water with ½ × 5ml tsp (½tsp) salt, 8 peppercorns, 1 sliced onion and a bouquet garni consisting of leek tops, parsley, thyme, bay leaf and a little fresh, or ¼ × 5ml tsp (¼tsp) dried, crushed fennel. Boil for about 30 min, strain and boil again for a little while.
2 Sauté remaining sliced onions and leeks in oil in another saucepan. Add boiling fish stock, wide strips of filleted fish and peeled, sliced tomatoes.
3 Cook for 6–8 min, add white wine and also heat the peeled shrimps without letting them boil. Season with salt and garnish with tiny sprigs of dill.

Salmon Pie –
Tourte de Saumon

(serves 4–6)
Preparation time: 20–25 min
Marinating time: 1 hr
Cooking time: about 40 min
Oven temperature: 220°C, 425°F,
Gas 7
Middle part of the oven
Unsuitable for the freezer

½–¾kg (about 1½lb) salmon
  (tailpiece) or sea trout
2 lemons
salt
butter
300g (11oz) puff pastry (homemade
  or frozen)
250g (9oz) mushrooms
pepper
200–300ml (7–10fl oz) sour cream
parsley
chives
1 egg

1 Clean fish and remove bones.
Divide into equal-sized pieces and
marinate for 1 hr in most of the
lemon juice.
2 Thaw the frozen pastry and roll
out to fit the top of an ovenproof
dish.
3 Clean the mushrooms, slice and
sauté in 15g (½oz) butter on strong
heat. Add salt and 1 × 15ml tbsp
(1tbsp) lemon juice, and boil until
all liquid has evaporated. Stir in
plenty of finely chopped parsley and
chives.
4 Place well-drained fish and mushrooms in an ovenproof dish. Whisk
egg. Mix together sour cream, a
dash of lemon juice, salt, pepper and
half the whisked egg. Spoon over
fish and cover with pastry.
Roll out left-over pastry and place a
strip round the edge of the dish.
Make a hole in the top to allow steam
to escape. Brush pastry with remaining whisked egg and bake as directed. Serve hot.

VARIATION
Use river trout, halibut or other
firm, but not too coarse, fish instead
of salmon. The fish can also be
baked completely enclosed, ie with
both a base and a top of pastry.
Allow about ½kg (1lb 2oz) pastry and
roll out the base and line the ovenproof dish before adding the other
ingredients. Use a metal dish if possible, so that the base bakes well.

Above: Salmon Pie. Below: Pollock or Cod with Peas.

Lumpfish from Normandy – Loup de Mer à la Normandie

(serves 6)
Preparation time: 30 min
Cooking time: about 50 min
Oven temperature: 200°C, 400°F, Gas 6
Middle part of the oven
Unsuitable for the freezer

1.2kg (2¾lb) lumpfish fillets
4 onions
salt, pepper
lemon juice
250g (9oz) mushrooms
butter
4 × 15ml tbsp (4tbsp) Calvados
   (apple liqueur)
about 400ml (¾pt) double cream
about 200ml (7fl oz) apple or white
   wine
200–300g (7–11oz) boiled mussels
6–8 crawfish tails

1 Rub fillets with salt, pepper and lemon juice. Cut into pieces, not too small, and place in a well-greased ovenproof dish along with 3 onions sliced into thin rings.
2 Chop remaining onion and slice mushrooms. Sauté in 25g (1oz) butter in a frying pan and season with salt and lemon juice. Pour Calvados over, heat everything briefly, and set alight. Shake frying pan until flames are extinguished and stir in about 200ml (7fl oz) cream. Remove sauce from the heat and season to taste with salt and freshly ground pepper.
3 Pour apple or white wine over the fish, then the mushroom sauce. Cover dish with tinfoil and bake in the oven for about 25 min. Remove tinfoil, spoon on remaining cream, and put thin flakes of butter over the top. Bake for further 10–15 min.
4 Carefully heat the shellfish in a little butter and lemon juice, and spoon over the dish.
Serve piping hot with boiled potatoes sprinkled with parsley. The flambéeing is optional, but it is this that gives the special flavour.
Brandy can be used as a substitute for Calvados, but any other spirit would kill the flavour. Shrimps can be used instead of crawfish tails. Allow 100g (¼lb), either fresh, canned or frozen.
The liquid from canned shellfish is a good substitute for the wine in the recipe.

Fit for a dinner party – Lumpfish from Normandy with mushrooms and onions.

Pollock or Cod with Peas – Colin aux Petits Pois

(serves 4)
Preparation time: 10–15 min
Cooking time: 20–25 min
Suitable for the freezer, but will lose some flavour

¾kg (1lb 10oz) pollock or cod with
   bones OR ½kg (1lb 2oz) filleted fish
salt
1kg (2¼lb) peas
butter, paprika
2 small parsnips
4 × 15ml tbsp (4tbsp) sultanas
100ml (4fl oz) dry white wine

1 Cut cleaned and skinned fish into pieces. Rub with a pinch of salt and leave for about 10 min.
2 Shell peas and parboil in lightly salted water. Keep warm. Peel parsnips, cut into small cubes and boil in lightly salted water for 6–8 min.
3 Dry fish slices well and sauté lightly in 15–25g (½–1oz) butter in a heavy casserole. Sprinkle with a little paprika. Add parsnip cubes, sultanas, wine and 100ml (4fl oz) water and cook carefully on low heat until everything is tender. Cooking time depends on the type of fish you use and the thickness of the slices or fillets. Finally add peas and season with salt. Serve hot with bread.
Instead of parsnips you can use potatoes or carrots. Frozen peas can be used instead of fresh – allow ½kg (1lb 2oz). Do not use canned peas. Sultanas have a slightly acid flavour and should not be replaced by raisins.

grated rind and juice of 1 lemon. Spoon over olives and the vegetable mixture.

4 Cover dish with tinfoil and bake as directed for about 30 min. Remove tinfoil when there is about 10 min left of cooking time and sprinkle with melted butter.

Dried Cod Casserole – Merluche à la Provençale
(serves 4)
This dish is made exactly as for Cod Casserole. Allow 400–500g (about 1lb) dried cod, steep for 24 hr, and remove skin and bones.
Cooking time is 45–60 min, depending on the thickness of the fish slices.

Scallops in Shells – Coquilles St Jacques
(serves 4)
Preparation time: 15 min
Cooking time: about 15 min
Top part of the oven
Unsuitable for the freezer

8 fresh scallops (clams)
2 shallots
butter
50g (2oz) salt pork or unsmoked
 bacon
200ml (7fl oz) dry white wine
100ml (4fl oz) cream
2 egg yolks
salt
pepper
grated Parmesan cheese
breadcrumbs
parsley

1 The edible part of the scallop is the firm, white lobe and the red coral. Discard everything else and scrub the scallop shells ready for serving.
2 Steam finely chopped shallot and finely chopped salt pork in 1 × 15ml tbsp (1tbsp) butter in a heavy casserole over low heat for about 5 min. Cut the white part of the scallops in two, place them in the casserole and add white wine. Cook, uncovered, on very low heat for 6–8 min.
3 Mix egg yolks with cream, add to casserole and stir over very low heat until sauce thickens, mixing in the coral and seasoning to taste with salt and pepper. Divide the mixture between 4 greased shells, sprinkle with chopped parsley and a couple of spoonsful of grated cheese and

Cod Casserole – Morue à la Provençale (above)
(serves 4)
Preparation time: 20–25 min
Cooking time: about 40 min
Oven temperature: 190–200°C, 375–400°F, Gas 5–6
Middle part of the oven
Unsuitable for the freezer

¾kg (1lb 10oz) cod slices
2 onions
2 cloves garlic
2 × 15ml tbsp (2tbsp) olive oil
15g (½oz) butter
1 lemon
4 tomatoes
1 head of fennel
3–4 stalks of celery OR *fennel tops*
150ml (¼pt) dry white wine
salt, pepper
paprika
50–100g (2–4oz) green olives

1 Rub cod slices with salt and leave in a cool place for about 15 min.
2 Sauté chopped onion and crushed garlic in the oil in a heavy casserole. Add peeled and quartered tomatoes, sliced celery or fennel top and finely sliced fennel base. Pour over white wine and simmer for about 5 min. Season with salt, pepper and paprika.
3 Place cod slices in a greased oven-proof dish. Sprinkle with finely

breadcrumbs. Brown under grill or on strong upper heat in the oven for a few minutes. Serve as a starter, or for lunch or supper.

If you can't get fresh scallops, you can use frozen. Add the sauce to the boiled scallops before browning. Scallops, fresh or frozen, must not be overcooked, or they will go tough.

Fish Stew with Tomatoes – Matelote Basque

(serves 6)
Preparation time: 30 min
Cooking time: about 20 min
Unsuitable for the freezer

¾kg (1lb 10oz) fillets of freshwater
   fish (pike, perch etc)
salt, pepper
juice of 1 lemon
200–300g (7–11oz) shallots
2 thin slices of bacon
olive oil
1–3 cloves garlic
6–8 tomatoes
300–400g (11–14oz) green beans
200ml (7fl oz) red wine
plain flour
butter
basil
parsley
dill

1 Sprinkle fish fillets with a little salt, squeeze the lemon juice over and leave in a cool place for 15–20 min. Peel shallots and cook until tender in lightly salted water. Scald, peel and halve tomatoes.

2 Cut bacon slices into small pieces and sauté for a couple of min in a saucepan in 1 × 15ml tbsp (1tbsp) olive oil. Add crushed garlic and 2–3 coarsely chopped, boiled shallots. Place tomato halves and sliced beans in the saucepan and simmer for 6–8 min.

3 Cut fish into bite-sized pieces and place in saucepan with remaining shallots. Add wine and simmer on low heat until fish is firm.

4 Mix 15g (½oz) softened butter with ½–1 × 15ml tbsp (½–1tbsp) plain flour. Stir carefully into saucepan, a little at a time, until sauce is smooth but not too thick. Season to taste with salt, pepper and fresh or dried herbs. Serve with a French loaf, rice, or sliced French loaf fried in oil to which crushed garlic has been added.

Above: Scallops in Shells. Below: Fish Stew with Tomatoes.

Hearty Fare from Alsace-Lorraine

Salt Pork and Vegetables – Potée Lorraine

(serves 6–8)
Preparation time: 30 min
Steeping time: 12 hr
Cooking time: about 2 hr
Meat, stock and vegetables are suitable for the freezer separately

200g (7oz) dried butter beans
1kg (2¼lb) lightly salted pork
1kg (2¼lb) bacon knuckle
½kg (1lb 2oz) smoked sausage
  (garlic flavour, if you prefer)
5–6 carrots
2 onions
1 bay leaf
celery leaves
1 sprig of thyme, parsley
peppercorns
1 small cabbage

1 Steep beans in cold water overnight. If pork is too salty, it should be left in water for a couple of hours.
2 Place pork and bacon in 1–1½ litres (1¼–2½pt) cold water, bring slowly to the boil and skim well. Simmer on low heat for about 1 hr.
3 Drain beans well and place them in the pot along with a bouquet garni of bay leaf, a few celery leaves, thyme and parsley. Peel carrots, peel and quarter onions and slice and add to pot with 1 × 5ml tsp (1tsp) peppercorns. Boil for about 40 min.
4 Remove bouquet garni and add smoked sausage and cabbage cut into large wedges. Add a little salt if necessary and boil until everything is tender.
Place meat and vegetables in separate dishes and pour over some of the stock. The remaining stock can be served as a clear gravy or frozen and used later. Serve dish piping hot with brown bread.

Smoked Loin of Pork with Horseradish Sauce – Schiffala Alsacienne

(serves 6)
Preparation time: 20 min
Cooking time: about 1½ hr
Suitable for the freezer

Left: Smoked Loin of Pork with Horseradish Sauce.

Above: Salt Pork and Vegetables – just the food for cold winter days.

1½kg (3lb) smoked loin of pork
1 large onion
2 cloves
2 carrots
a few celery leaves
40g (1½oz) fresh white breadcrumbs
300ml (½pt) double cream
salt, parsley (optional)
pepper, grated horseradish

1 Place meat in plenty of cold water, bring to the boil and skim well. Stud the onion with the cloves and add to the casserole with the carrots and a few celery leaves. Simmer on low heat for about 40 min. Remove from heat and leave meat in the water for 45–50 min.
2 To make the horseradish sauce, remove cloves and finely chop the onion. Mix in breadcrumbs and cream, stirring well together. Add grated horseradish, salt and pepper to taste. Slice meat and place on a serving dish. Garnish with parsley or a little freshly grated horseradish. Serve hot or cold, with the cold horseradish sauce and brown bread.

1

A Classic Recipe

Boeuf à la Mode is a French culinary classic — equally popular as a family, and as a party, dish. It can be served either hot or cold. You need not be a cordon bleu cook to prepare it — just wanting to have a go and using the right ingredients will ensure you a successful meal.

French Braised Beef – Boeuf à la Mode
(serves 8)
Preparation time: 30 min
Marinating time: 6–8 hr
Cooking time: 2½–3 hr
Oven temperature: 220° and 180°C, 425° and 350°F, Gas 7 and 4
Bottom part of the oven
Suitable for the freezer, but will lose some flavour

2kg (4½lb) lean boned beef
about 200g (7oz) thinly sliced fat
40g (1½oz) butter
3 × 15ml tbsp (3tbsp) flour
salt, pepper
8 ripe tomatoes
400ml (¾pt) good stock
3 × 15ml tbsp (3tbsp) tomato purée
Marinade: 2 carrots
3 onions
1 clove garlic
2 stalks of celery
3 bay leaves
1 sprig of parsley
3 sprigs of thyme
3 × 15ml tbsp (3tbsp) brandy
¾–1 litre (1¼–1¾pt) bottle dark, heavy red wine
Trimmings: ½kg (1lb 2oz) small onions
1kg (2¼lb) carrots
100g (¼lb) butter
2–3 × 15ml tbsp (2–3tbsp) sugar (optional)

1 The marinating is very important for a successful result — it makes the meat tender and juicy, and gives it a good flavour. If the marinade does not cover the meat completely, the latter will have to be turned or basted.

2

3

2 Peeled tomatoes and gravy are added to the roasting tin when the meat is brown. Herbs and vegetables which have been in the marinade will also add a piquant flavour to the meat.

3 Small onions and carrot sticks can either be browned or glazed, according to taste. Glaze by boiling butter and sugar together to form a bubbling syrup. Add the vegetables and stir carefully for a few minutes until they are brown and shiny.

1 Dry and trim meat. Cover with large thin pieces of fat, and fasten these with toothpicks. Or you can bard the meat with a barding needle. Put the strips of fat in the fridge for a couple of hours before barding, so that they are easier to pull through the meat.

2 Make marinade by slicing the vegetables and combining with the crushed garlic, herbs, brandy and red wine. Place the meat in this and leave for 6–8 hr, turning fairly often.

3 Remove meat, dry well and sprinkle with salt and coarsely ground pepper. Place in a small roasting tin or ovenproof dish and brown for 20–30 min at 220°C, 425°F, Gas 7.

4 Make gravy while meat is in the oven by melting the 40g (1½oz) butter in a thick-bottomed saucepan, adding the flour and stirring continuously until the mixture is light brown. Add strained marinade and stock alternately, until the gravy is thick and smooth. Boil on low heat for about 10 min. Add tomato purée, and season with salt and pepper.

5 Take roasting tin out of the oven and pour off the melted fat. Pour gravy into roasting tin. Scald and peel tomatoes and place in tin, and add herbs and vegetables from marinade. As soon as the gravy is boiling in the roasting tin, lower heat to 180°C, 350°F, Gas 4. Leave meat in oven for 2–2½ hr, basting often with the gravy. The roast can alternatively be covered with tinfoil or other cover — then you do not have to baste.

6 Peel the onions for the trimmings, scrape and slice the carrots. Boil vegetables until nearly tender in lightly salted water, then drain. Sauté the onion and carrots in the

butter, or glaze them in butter and 2–3 × 15ml tbsp (2–3tbsp) sugar. Turn off heat, but leave roast for a while in the oven. Remove herbs but not the tomatoes. Bring gravy to boil and season again if necessary, or add a few drops of brandy. Slice roast, place on a hot serving dish and pour gravy over. Garnish with the onions and carrots. Serve the remaining gravy in a gravy boat. Accompany with boiled potatoes.

VARIATION
Boeuf à la Mode is often served cold. The procedure is then somewhat different. Marinate the meat, but without using brandy. Dry meat and brown in butter in a casserole with onion from the marinade. Pour brandy over and flambé. Add seasoning, purée, stock and marinade. Place a tight-fitting lid on casserole and leave in oven at 150°C, 300°F, Gas 2 for about 4 hr.

Remove meat and strain meat juices. Cool and remove surface layer of fat. Slice the cold meat and place the slices together to look as if one whole piece. Place small onions and carrots (browned or plain boiled) around the meat. Dissolve gelatine – 8g ($\frac{1}{4}$oz) to 200ml (7fl oz) liquid – in some of the heated meat juices. Stir in the rest of the meat juices and sprinkle the half-set gelatine over the meat and vegetables.

Sunday Lunch from Provence

Provence is well-known for beautiful scenery, good wines and excellent food.

Sunday lunch consists of four courses, as in the following menu and recipes.

Anchovy Sandwiches
Tournedos with Green Beans
Cheese with Country-style Bread
Fresh Fruit

Country-style Bread
(makes 2 loaves)

1kg (2¼lb) flour
3 × 5ml tsp (3tsp) salt
4 × 15ml tbsp (4tbsp) oil
2 eggs
egg or flour for tops
50g (2oz) yeast
500ml (1pt) lukewarm water

1 Dissolve the yeast in a little lukewarm water and thoroughly mix in all the ingredients.
2 Leave dough to rise for ½–1 hr.
3 Divide into two and shape each half to a round. Leave to rise for further 30 min.
4 Score the tops with a sharp knife and brush with egg or sprinkle with a little flour. Bake at 200–220°C, 400–425°F, Gas 6–7 for about 25 min. Cool on a wire rack.

Anchovy Sandwiches –
Croûtes Provençales
(serves 6)
Preparation time: 20 min
Cooking time: about 20 min
Unsuitable for the freezer

2 onions
4 tomatoes
3–4 × 15ml tbsp (3–4tbsp) olive oil
1 green pepper
salt, pepper
black olives
thyme, butter (optional)
6 anchovy fillets
2 × 15ml tbsp (2tbsp) breadcrumbs
6 slices of white sandwich loaf
2 × 15ml tbsp (2tbsp) grated
  Gruyère cheese

1 Sauté coarsely chopped onion in 2 × 15ml tbsp (2tbsp) oil until lightly golden. Add deseeded, thinly sliced pepper and scalded and peeled tomatoes cut into four. Add salt, pepper and 1 × 5ml tsp (1tsp) fresh, or ½ × 5ml tsp (½tsp) dried, thyme. Simmer until they form a soft purée.
2 Fry the crustless bread slices in remaining oil or butter, and place in an ovenproof dish. Divide vegetable mixture between the slices. Add anchovy fillets and olives. Sprinkle with the grated cheese and breadcrumbs. Brown under grill or strong upper heat for a few minutes.

Tournedos with Green Beans –
Tournedos aux Haricots Verts
(serves 6)
Preparation time: 15 min
Cooking time: 6–8 min
Cooking beans: 15 min
Unsuitable for the freezer

6 slices fillet of beef 3–4cm (1–1½in)
  thick
6 slices of fresh fat
2 × 15ml tbsp (2tbsp) olive oil
salt, pepper
1 × 5ml tsp (1tsp) mixed herbs
150–250ml (5–9fl oz) red wine
about 150g (5oz) butter
1kg (2¼lb) green beans
1–2 cloves garlic
finely chopped parsley

1 Shape meat slices until nice and round and tie the slices of fat around them. Brush the meat surface with oil and rub with coarsely ground black pepper and herbs. Let meat rest for about 10 min.
2 Prepare the beans and cook, uncovered, in boiling, salted water until tender.
3 Place steaks in a very hot, dry iron frying pan. Brown them quickly on both sides. Add about 50g (2oz) butter, lower heat, and fry for about 3 min each side. Sprinkle steaks with salt and place on a hot serving dish. Deglaze frying pan with red wine and stir in about 75g (3oz) butter. Pour meat juices around meat.
4 Drain beans and steam them for a moment in melted butter with the crushed garlic and 2 × 15ml tbsp (2tbsp) parsley. Serve with baked or fried potatoes and French bread.

Tasty Beef and Pork Dishes

Good ingredients and careful preparation is the secret of a successful meal. The French housewife knows this. She takes her time shopping and puts both consideration and love into her cooking.
Here are five delicious meat dishes to delight any gourmet.

**Braised Beef with Corn Purée –
Rôti de Boeuf au Purée de Maïs**
(serves 6)
Preparation time: 30 min
Cooking time: 25–35 min
Oven temperature: 220–230°C, 425–450°F, Gas 7–8
Bottom half of the oven
Unsuitable for the freezer

1kg (2¼lb) slices of beef
100g (¼lb) bacon
2 onions
1 yellow and 1 green pepper
6 tomatoes
1 clove garlic
50g (2oz) butter
salt, pepper
300ml (½pt) stock

300ml (½pt) red wine
1 bay leaf
paprika

1 Cut bacon into very small cubes and sauté in a frying pan until the fat runs. Add chopped onions, de-seeded and chopped peppers, 1 chopped tomato and crushed garlic. Simmer for a couple of min.
2 Rub beef slices with coarsely ground black pepper and brown on both sides in butter in a heavy casserole or deep frying pan. Use an iron pot only if it has been specially treated, for red wine and tomatoes affect the iron in the old-fashioned types of pot and the food takes on a rather repulsive colour.

Sprinkle with salt, place the cooked vegetables around and pour in 200ml (7fl oz) stock and 50ml (2fl oz) red wine. Place casserole in pre-heated oven for about 20 min.

3 Scald, peel and chop remaining tomatoes. Simmer for about 10 min with the remaining stock and red wine, salt, pepper, crumbled bay leaf, and paprika to taste. Add to the meat and cook casserole for 5–15 min, depending on how rare you want your meat.

Serve meat sliced, with its tomato-flavoured gravy. Accompany with boiled rice, a green salad and corn purée.

To boil rice: Sauté long-grain rice in a little butter and 1–1½ × 5ml tsp

(1–1½tsp) turmeric until the rice ceases to be transparent, but do not brown. Add water, and boil rice according to directions on the packet. Add small cubes of red pepper near the end of the cooking time.

Corn Purée – Purée de Maïs
Preparation time: 15 min
Cooking time: about 40 min
Unsuitable for the freezer

4–6 cobs of corn
salt, pepper
2 shallots
½ green pepper
25g (1oz) butter
2–3 × 15ml tbsp (2–3tbsp) grated
*   cheese*
100ml (4fl oz) single cream
2 egg yolks
paprika

1 Place cobs in boiling, lightly salted water and boil until tender. Time of cooking depends on how ripe the cobs are. Scrape the kernels off with a knife and mash with a fork.
2 Sauté coarsely chopped shallots and deseeded, chopped pepper in butter on low heat for 5 min. Stir in mashed corn and boil for a couple of min, stirring constantly.
3 Mix cream and egg yolks with 1 × 5ml tsp (1tsp) paprika and the grated cheese. Stir into the hot corn mixture but do not allow to boil. Season again, if necessary.

VARIATION
Instead of corn purée you can serve green pea purée, made with fresh peas when possible.

Green Pea Purée – Purée de Petits Pois
Sauté 2 small onions in 1 × 15ml tbsp (1tbsp) butter with 2 finely shredded lettuce leaves. Add about 400g (14oz) shelled peas, 200–300ml (7–10fl oz) water and 1 × 5ml tsp (1tsp) salt. Boil, uncovered, until peas are tender. Add more water if necessary, but when

peas are ready you should have no more than a couple of spoonsful of water left in the saucepan. Rub everything through a sieve and blend purée on low heat with 1 × 15ml tbsp (1tbsp) butter. Season with salt and pepper and sprinkle with a little finely chopped parsley.

Stuffed Meat Rolls – Paupiettes de Porc à la Bière
(serves 4)
Preparation time: 20 min
Cooking time: about 1 hr
Suitable for the freezer in the meat juices

4 slices of pork
2 slices of bread
4 × 15ml tbsp (4tbsp) milk
2 onions
parsley
chervil
pork dripping or butter
6–8 shallots
salt, pepper
nutmeg
400–500ml (¾–1pt) beer (Pilsner or
*   non-alcoholic)*
1 bay leaf
1 sprig of thyme

1 Slap meat lightly with the back of the hand and sprinkle with salt and pepper. Soak bread, crusts removed, in the milk.
2 Sauté chopped onion in 15g (½oz) pork dripping or butter and mix with the bread, 2–3 × 15ml tbsp (2–3tbsp) finely chopped parsley and 1–2 × 15ml tbsp (1–2tbsp) chervil. Season to taste.
3 Spread the stuffing on the meat slices, roll them up and tie with cotton. Sauté the rolls in butter or dripping in a heavy casserole. Sprinkle with nutmeg and add beer, bay leaf and thyme. Simmer, covered, for about 45 min.
4 Peel the shallots, place in casserole and continue to simmer until everything is cooked.

Serve with white bread and spinach.

See illustration overleaf.

Meatballs with Spring Vegetables – Boulettes de Viande aux Printanière

(serves 4)
Preparation time: 30 min
Cooking time: about 45 min
Suitable for the freezer

½kg (1lb 2oz) boneless veal or pork
100g (¼lb) smoked ham
salt, pepper
3 × 15ml tbsp (3tbsp) breadcrumbs
100ml (4fl oz) stock
6 small new carrots
6 small onions
2–3 turnips
25g (½oz) butter
3–4 × 15ml tbsp (3–4tbsp) tomato
   purée
cabbage leaves (see method)

1 Mince meat and ham together. Add 1 × 5ml tsp (1tsp) salt and breadcrumbs steeped in the stock. Stir well until the mixture is smooth and firm. Add pepper and shape into balls.
2 Scrape carrots, peel onions and peel and slice turnips. Boil in 300ml (½pt) water with the butter and ½–1 × 5ml tsp (½–1tsp) salt. Remove vegetables and boil as many cabbage leaves as meatballs in the stock. Remove and boil the meatballs in the stock for 20 min.
3 Wrap meatballs in cabbage leaves. Add tomato purée and seasoning to stock, add vegetables and meatballs and heat well.
Serve with baked potatoes or chips.

Beef in Tangy Sauce – Boeuf à la Moutarde de Dijon

(serves 6)
Preparation time: 20 min
Cooking time: about 20 min
Suitable for the freezer, but will lose some flavour

1kg (2¼lb) fillet or rump
1 × 15ml tbsp (1tbsp) plain flour
250ml (9fl oz) stock
1 × 5ml tsp (1tsp) Dijon mustard
1 × 15ml tbsp (1tbsp) tomato purée
3 onions
40g (1½oz) butter
salt, black pepper
paprika
100–200ml (4–7fl oz) double cream
   or sour cream

Above: Stuffed Meat Rolls. Below: Meatballs with Spring Vegetables.

1 Blend flour and stock together in a thick-bottomed saucepan, bring to the boil and add mustard, tomato purée, salt and pepper. Simmer for about 10 min on low heat, stirring from time to time.

2 Sauté chopped onion in 25g (1oz) butter, add to the sauce and boil for a couple of min. Cut meat into small slices across the fibres, sauté in 15g (½oz) butter on high heat and sprinkle with salt and pepper. Place in sauce.

3 Add ½–1 × 15ml tbsp (½–1tbsp) paprika mixed with cream or sour cream. Heat through and season to taste with salt if necessary.

Serve with potato purée or boiled potatoes with lightly whisked sour cream on top.

Beef Casserole from the Camargue – Boeuf à la Gardiane

(serves 6)
Preparation time: 20 min
Cooking time: 2½–3 hr
Suitable for the freezer

1kg (2¼lb) stewing beef
25g (½oz) butter
1–2 × 15ml tbsp (1–2tbsp) oil
salt, pepper
4 tomatoes
4–5 onions
1 clove garlic
2 bay leaves
1 sprig of thyme
1 sprig of parsley
250–300ml (9–10fl oz) red or white wine
10–12 black olives

1 Cut meat into cubes and sauté in butter and oil. Season with salt and pepper and place in a heavy casserole.

2 Scald, peel and quarter tomatoes. Lightly sauté onions and crushed garlic and add vegetables to casserole with a bouquet garni of bay leaves, thyme and parsley.

3 Add wine and simmer, covered, on low heat. Or place casserole in oven preheated to 180°C, 350°F, Gas 4. When ½ hr remains of the cooking time, add coarsely chopped stoned olives. Remove bouquet garni and serve with boiled potatoes or rice.

Above : Beef Casserole from the Camargue. Below : Beef in Tangy Sauce.

1 Cut ham into small cubes or strips and place in a bowl with chopped shallots, crushed garlic, 3–4 × 15ml tbsp (3–4tbsp) finely chopped parsley and 8–10 coarsely crushed peppercorns. Pour on white wine and leave bowl, covered, in a cool place overnight.

2 Roll out puff pastry to make one large and one smaller round, to fit an ovenproof dish or baking tin. Rinse dish or tin with cold water and place the largest pastry circle at the bottom and up along the sides.

3 Drain ham and place in pastry case. Mash cream cheese and beat until smooth with egg and a little wine from the marinade. Season to taste with salt, pepper and finely chopped parsley. Spread over the ham filling.

4 Place the other puff pastry circle on top and press the edges together. Alternatively place a thin strip of pastry round the edge. Cut a whole in the top to allow steam to escape and place a thin strip of dough around the hole. Brush with egg yolk and bake as directed.

Chicken Liver Pâté –
Mousse de Foie de Volaille
(makes about ½kg [1lb 2oz])
Preparation time: 30 min
Unsuitable for the freezer

400g (14oz) chicken's liver
  (optionally mixed with duck, goose
  or other bird liver)
75g (3oz) butter
1 shallot
4 × 15ml tbsp (4tbsp) dry sherry or
  Madeira
salt, black pepper, paprika
¼ × 5ml tsp (¼tsp) dried herbs
1 egg white

1 Rinse and dry liver and remove any membranes. Slice, and sauté in 15g (½oz) butter for about 3 min on strong heat.

2 Lower heat and add grated or finely chopped shallot, salt, pepper, paprika and wine. Allow mixture to sizzle for 1 min, then press through a sieve or purée in a blender.

3 Beat remaining butter into the pâté, add dried herbs and adjust seasoning if necessary. Cool for a short while and carefully mix in the stiffly whisked egg white. Spoon into a dish and leave, covered, in a cold place overnight.

Country Classics

Ham Pie –
Pâté Lorraine (above)
(serves 6)
Preparation time: 20 min
Marinating time: 12 hr
Cooking time: about 45 min
Oven temperature: 220–230°C, 425–450°F, Gas 7–8
Bottom or middle part of the oven
Can be frozen uncooked

400–500g (about 1lb) puff pastry
  (for homemade see recipe, or use
  frozen)
1 egg yolk for brushing
Filling :
300–400g (11–14oz) boiled ham
4 shallots
1 clove garlic
100ml (4fl oz) dry white wine
parsley, pepper
salt, peppercorns
100g (¼lb) cream cheese
1 egg

Pig's Liver Pâté flavoured with juniper berries.

Puff Pastry

Mix 250g (9oz) plain flour to a smooth dough with 100–150ml (4–5fl oz) cold water and a pinch of salt. Leave in a cold place for at least 1 hr, then roll out to a rectangle.

Cut 200g (7oz) butter into thin slices and place across $\frac{2}{3}$ of the pastry. Fold the one-third not covered with butter across the butter-covered part and the last third over this. Leave in a cold place for at least another 1 hr.

Roll out pastry to form a rectangle, being careful that the butter does not come through and stick to the work surface or the rolling pin. Fold into three as before and leave in a cold place for 1 hr. Repeat rolling out and folding another 2–3 times, giving pastry a $\frac{1}{4}$ turn at each rolling out (make a mark at the edge of the folded pastry to indicate which side you are going to have nearest you next time). After the final rolling out, the pastry is ready for use.

Frozen Puff Pastry

Thaw as instructed on packet. As with homemade puff pastry, be careful to roll out evenly so that the pastry rises the same amount all over in cooking.

Pig's Liver Pâté –
Terrine de Foie de Porc

(makes about $1\frac{1}{2}$kg [3lb])
Preparation time: 30 min
Cooking time: about $1\frac{1}{2}$ hr
Oven temperature: 160°C, 325°F, Gas 3
Bottom part of the oven
Uncooked, is suitable for the freezer

$\frac{1}{2}$kg (1lb 2oz) pig's liver
250g (9oz) pork
250g (9oz) lean veal
3 onions
1 clove garlic
1 thick slice of bread
100ml (4fl oz) dry white wine
salt, powdered cloves

thyme, pepper
4–5 juniper berries (optional)
2 eggs
about 200g (7oz) sliced fat

1 Put liver, pork, veal and onions once through a mincer. Mix well together with crustless bread soaked in white wine. Add crushed garlic, 1–$1\frac{1}{2} \times 5$ml tsp (1–$1\frac{1}{2}$tsp) salt, $\frac{1}{4} \times 5$ml tsp ($\frac{1}{4}$tsp) pepper, $\frac{1}{4} \times 5$ml tsp ($\frac{1}{4}$tsp) cloves, $\frac{1}{4} \times 5$ml tsp ($\frac{1}{4}$tsp) crushed thyme and crushed juniper berries. Whisk the eggs and stir in.

2 Place thin slices of fat in a deep ovenproof dish in such a way that they reach about half way up the sides. Spoon in mince and fold fat slices over. Bake as directed and pull the fat away from the sides a little during the last 15–20 min of cooking time. Cool in the dish. Serve cold with bread, olives, sour cherries or small pickled gherkins and beetroots.

dish and pour heated brandy over. Set alight and allow flames to burn themselves out.

3 Add red wine and a bouquet garni consisting of 3 sprigs of parsley, 1 sprig of thyme and 2 bay leaves. Cover and cook in oven for about 40 min, basting meat from time to time.

4 Sauté whole, peeled mushrooms in 8g ($\frac{1}{4}$oz) butter and $\frac{1}{2} \times 15$ml tbsp ($\frac{1}{2}$tbsp) oil and season with salt. Stir carefully into dish and cook for a further 10–15 min to make the meat browner. Remove bouquet garni.

5 Mix together 15g ($\frac{1}{2}$oz) butter and the plain flour and stir carefully into the meat juices along with the crushed garlic. Season to taste with salt and pepper and leave dish in the oven for a further 5 min. Sprinkle with parsley and serve with butter-fried bread cubes.

Chicken Savoy – Poulet à la Savoyarde

(serves 4)
Preparation time: 20 min
Cooking time: about 1 hr
Oven temperature: 220°C, 425°F, Gas 7
Middle part of the oven
Suitable for the freezer without topping of cheese and breadcrumbs

1 large chicken
salt, pepper
parsley, tarragon
butter
2 small onions
250ml (9fl oz) stock
100ml (4fl oz) white wine
grated cheese
200ml (7fl oz) double cream
2 × 5ml tsp (2tsp) French mustard
breadcrumbs
flour

1 Divide chicken into 4 pieces, rub with salt and pepper, and spread on about 25g (1oz) butter. Place pieces

Chicken in Wine – Coq au Vin (above)

(serves 5–6)
Preparation time: 30 min
Cooking time: about 1 hr
Oven temperature: 190–200°C, 375–400°F, Gas 5–6
Bottom part of the oven
Unsuitable for the freezer

1 young meaty chicken
2 slices pork
250g (9oz) small onions
250g (9oz) mushrooms
pepper, salt
butter
olive oil
4 × 15ml tbsp (4tbsp) brandy

½ bottle good red wine
2 cloves garlic
parsley
1 sprig of thyme
2 bay leaves
1 × 15ml tbsp (1tbsp) plain flour

1 Divide chicken into 6–8 pieces. Cut pork into small cubes and fry in 15g ($\frac{1}{2}$oz) butter and $\frac{1}{2} \times 15$ml tbsp ($\frac{1}{2}$tbsp) oil. Remove pork cubes from frying pan and sauté whole, peeled onions in the fat. Place pork and onions in an ovenproof dish.

2 Add some more butter to the frying pan. Rub chicken pieces with salt and pepper and brown on all sides. Add pieces to the ovenproof

in an ovenproof dish with 1 sprig of parsley, 3–4 sprigs of fresh, or $\frac{1}{2} \times 5$ml tsp ($\frac{1}{2}$tsp) dried, tarragon and peeled onions. Pour over 100ml (4fl oz) stock and place dish in oven. Cook for about 50 min, basting from time to time.

2 Melt 25g (1oz) butter for the sauce. Stir in 2×15ml tbsp (2tbsp) plain flour and then remaining stock, wine and cream. Add mustard, 1×15ml tbsp (1tbsp) cheese, salt and pepper.

3 Place chicken in another ovenproof dish. Strain meat juices and stir into sauce. Pour sauce over chicken. Sprinkle with 2×15ml tbsp (2tbsp) grated cheese mixed with 2×15ml tbsp (2tbsp) breadcrumbs and place dish in oven until surface is golden. Serve with bread and salad.

Chicken Marengo (right)
Poulet Sauté à la Marengo
(serves 4)
Preparation time: 20 min
Cooking time: about 45 min
Unsuitable for the freezer

2 small chickens
3×15ml tbsp (3tbsp) oil
150g (5oz) small onions
200g (7oz) mushrooms
salt
pepper
1 clove garlic
2 tomatoes
150ml ($\frac{1}{4}$pt) white wine
250ml (9fl oz) stock
1 bay leaf
flour
a few black peppercorns

1 Divide each chicken into four. Heat the oil in a frying pan, season the chicken pieces and sauté well for about 15 min. Remove from pan. Clean mushrooms and peel onions, but leave them whole. Sauté until brown in same pan, then

remove.
2 Scald, peel and chop tomatoes. Sauté in the pan together with crushed garlic, without browning. Sprinkle with flour and stir in white wine, stock, crushed bay leaf and peppercorns. Return chicken to pan and simmer with the other ingredients for about 20 min.
3 Remove chicken pieces and strain the sauce through a sieve. Pour sauce into a saucepan, add browned onions and simmer, covered, until onions are tender.
4 Add mushrooms and chicken pieces and heat thoroughly before serving. Sprinkle with parsley and serve with rice.

French Cheeses
In France, cheese is always served before the dessert, along with fresh Country-style Bread (see page 33) or French loaf (baguette), without butter. The cheeses selected depend on individual taste, but both mild and strong varieties should be served. There are many to choose from – Brie, Camembert, Port Salut, French Emmenthaler, Roquefort, Saint-Paulin, to name but a few. Arrange the cheeses on a tray or a bread-board and, if you like, put a name on each one. Provide at least two knives – one for the mild, and one for the strong, cheeses.

Vegetable Dishes

The French have a great inventiveness when it comes to cooking vegetables. And now that such a wide range of imported vegetables is available in our own shops, we can follow their lead.

Above : Courgettes in Yoghurt (for recipe, see page 44).

**Aubergines with Cheese and Tomato –
Aubergines au Gratin**
(serves 4)
Preparation time: 15 min
Salting time: 30–45 min
Frying time: about 35 min
Unsuitable for the freezer

2 medium-sized aubergines (egg
  plants)
salt, pepper
6 tomatoes
parsley, thyme, basil
1 onion
olive oil
grated cheese

1 Wash the aubergines. If the skin
is thick and tough, it is better
to peel them. Slice lengthways,
sprinkle with coarse salt and place
in a sieve or colander.
2 Scald and peel tomatoes and cut
into pieces. Steam for about 20 min
in 1 × 15ml tbsp (1tbsp) oil with
chopped onion, 2 sprigs of parsley
and a sprig of thyme and basil.
Rub tomatoes through a sieve and
season purée to taste with salt and
pepper. This is called Coulis de
Tomate – the homemade tomato
sauce used in many French dishes.
3 Dry aubergine slices and sauté, a

few at a time if necessary, in
2–3 × 15ml tbsp (2–3tbsp) oil on
constant heat. Divide between individual ovenproof dishes and pour
tomato sauce on top. Sprinkle with
plenty of grated cheese and brown
under grill until melted and golden.
Serve hot as a first course or as
a vegetable to accompany roast
poultry or other meat dishes.
Alternatively, serve cold as a first
course.

**Carrots with Pork –
Carottes au Lard** (left)
(serves 4)
Preparation time: 15 min
Cooking time: about 15 min
Unsuitable for the freezer

½kg (1lb 2oz) small carrots
10–12 shallots or small onions
about 200g (7oz) lean pork
40g (1½oz) butter
salt, pepper

Cold or hot, Aubergines with Cheese
and Tomato are delicious.

200–300ml (7–10fl oz) stock
parsley

1 Rinse and scrape carrots and cut
into pieces. Peel the shallots. If
there are any green sprouts, chop
finely to sprinkle on dish when
cooked.
2 Cut pork into small cubes and
sauté lightly, in a saucepan, in 15g
(½oz) butter. Add carrots and
onions and fry for a couple of minutes. Sprinkle with salt and
pepper.
3 Add stock, bring to the boil and
simmer, with the lid on, until vegetables are tender and liquid has
evaporated. Stir in remaining
butter and sprinkle with finely
chopped parsley.
Serve as a separate course, or with
fried meats.

43

Left: Chicory with Ham is a really tasty hot dish when served with bread and a green salad.

large mushrooms and peel caps. Place mushrooms in a sieve as you wash them, so that they do not soak up the water.

2 Melt butter in a large, shallow saucepan or frying pan. Slice mushrooms and place in pan. Shake pan and add a pinch of salt, white pepper, finely chopped shallots, dash of grated nutmeg and finely chopped parsley.

3 Cook over moderate heat, turning carefully. Sprinkle with lemon juice. Add cream and continue to cook for a couple of min. Season again with salt, if necessary.

Serve as a separate course with butter-fried slices of white bread, or as accompaniment to veal, mutton or poultry.

Chicory (Belgian Endive) with Ham –
Endives en Pochon

(serves 4)
Preparation time: 20 min
Cooking time: about 30 min
Oven temperature: 200 °C, 400 °F, Gas 6
Unsuitable for the freezer

6–8 medium-sized heads of chicory
3 onions
100–200g (4–7oz) cooked ham
50g (2oz) butter
100ml (4fl oz) white wine
2–3 × 15ml tbsp (2–3tbsp) tomato purée
3 eggs
salt, pepper
parsley
50–75g (2–3oz) grated cheese

1 Remove any withered or damaged leaves from the chicory and cut off the small root stalk with a sharp knife.

2 Steam chicory until nearly tender in lightly salted water, then drain well. Place in a greased ovenproof dish.

3 Sauté chopped onions in the butter until lightly golden and add coarsely chopped ham, white wine and tomato purée. Turn off the heat and stir in eggs whisked with salt, pepper and 1 × 15ml tbsp (1tbsp) finely chopped parsley.

4 Pour mixture into dish and

Courgettes in Yoghurt –
Courgettes au Yogourt

(serves 4)
Preparation time: 10 min
Salting time: 30–45 min
Cooking time: about 15 min
Unsuitable for the freezer

½kg (1lb 2oz) small courgettes
salt, pepper, butter
300–400ml (½–¾pt) natural yoghurt
about 100g (¼lb) grated cheese

1 Wash the courgettes, but do not peel. Cut lengthways, sprinkle with salt, and leave on kitchen paper with the cut side down for 30–45 min.

2 Dry courgettes and slice or cut into sticks. Steam until tender, but not for too long, in steaming, lightly salted water. Drain in a colander.

3 Well grease an ovenproof dish and place in courgettes. Stir yoghurt with salt and pepper to taste

and pour over. Sprinkle with grated cheese and place dish under grill until cheese is golden.

Serve as a separate course with French bread, or with meat dishes.

Mushrooms in Cream Sauce –
Champignons à la Crème

(serves 4)
Preparation time: 15 min
Cooking time: about 15 min
Unsuitable for the freezer

½kg (1lb 2oz) mushrooms
25g (1oz) butter
salt, pepper
2 shallots
grated nutmeg
2 × 15ml tbsp (2tbsp) finely chopped parsley
1 × 15ml tbsp (1tbsp) lemon juice
100–200ml (4–7fl oz) double cream

1 Rub button mushrooms clean, or gently wash. Trim end of stalks of

sprinkle with grated cheese. Bake as directed. Serve hot as a separate coarse with white bread and a green salad.

Mushrooms Bordeaux-style – Champignons à la Bordelaise

(serves 4)
Preparation time: 10 min
Cooking time: 4–5 min
Unsuitable for the freezer

250g (9oz) fresh mushrooms
2 × 15ml tbsp (2tbsp) olive oil
parsley
1 shallot
1–2 cloves garlic
salt, pepper
2–3 × 15ml tbsp (2–3tbsp)
  breadcrumbs

1 Slice cleaned or peeled mushrooms and sauté in the oil for 2 min.
2 Lower heat and add 2–3 × 15ml tbsp (2–3tbsp) finely chopped pars-

ley, finely chopped shallot, crushed garlic, breadcrumbs and salt and pepper to taste.
3 Continue to cook for a few minutes, adding more salt if necessary. Serve hot on toast as a first course, or as a garnish with meat dishes.

Mushrooms with Onions – Champignons aux Oignons

(above)
(serves 4–6)
Preparation time: 20 min
Cooking time: about 40 min
Unsuitable for the freezer

300–400g (11–14oz) fresh
  mushrooms
4–5 ripe tomatoes
1 × 15ml tbsp (1tbsp) olive oil
salt
200–300ml (7–10fl oz) dry white
  wine
3 bay leaves
6 peppercorns
1 sprig of thyme
1 lemon
10 fairly small onions

1 Clean button mushrooms separately under cold, running water, but do not allow to remain in the water. Place in a bowl and sprinkle with lemon juice to prevent discoloration. Peel larger mushrooms.
2 Scald, peel and slice tomatoes. Put in a saucepan with olive oil, salt, peppercorns, 1 bay leaf and thyme, and cook until very soft. Rub through a fine-meshed sieve or purée in a blender. Pour purée back into saucepan.
3 Place whole peeled onions in the saucepan. Boil for 10 min, then add mushrooms, white wine and 2 bay leaves. Boil for about 10 min on low heat with the lid on. Season again if necessary.
Served hot as a separate vegetable dish it is enough for 4.

Cauliflower Polonaise – Chou-fleur à la Polonaise
(left)
(serves 4)
Preparation time: 10 min
Cooking time: 10–15 min
Unsuitable for the freezer

1 large cauliflower
salt
3–4 eggs
100g (¼lb) butter
about 4 × 15ml tbsp (4tbsp)
breadcrumbs

1 Trim cauliflower, rinse well in water and boil in lightly salted water, either whole or in sprigs.
2 Meanwhile hard boil the eggs, peel and coarsely chop. Sauté breadcrumbs until golden.
3 Drain cauliflower well and place on a hot serving dish. Sprinkle half the eggs over and pour butter mixed with breadcrumbs on top.

Black Salsify in Cream Sauce – Salsifis Noir à la Crème
(serves 4)
Salsify (oyster plant) is a long, thin root whose soft, white delicious flesh is said to taste of oysters – hence its name. The black-skinned variety (scorzonera) used in this recipe has better flavour.
Preparation time: 15 min
Cooking time: 15–25 min
Suitable for the freezer, but will lose some flavour

½kg (1lb 2oz) black salsify
salt, pepper
vinegar
25g (1oz) butter
1–1½ × 15ml tbsp (1–1½tbsp) plain
flour
200–300ml (7–10fl oz) stock
parsley
100ml (4fl oz) double cream or sour
cream

1 Scrape or peel the roots, putting them in vinegar water to prevent the flesh from going dark. Transfer to boiling, lightly salted water and cook until tender, but not mushy.
2 Meanwhile make the sauce by mixing softened butter and flour and cooking for a couple of minutes without browning. Gradually add the stock. Boil for a couple of minutes and stir in cream or sour cream. Season to taste.

3 Place drained roots on a hot serving dish, pour sauce over and sprinkle with a little finely chopped parsley.

Leeks with Ham – Poireaux au Jambon (below)
(serves 4)
Preparation time: 10–15 min
Cooking time: about 20 min
Suitable for the freezer, but will lose some flavour

6–8 medium sized leeks
2 shallots
150–200g (5–7oz) cooked ham
salt, pepper
butter
wine vinegar
200–300ml (7–10fl oz) double cream
finely chopped parsley

1 Wash and clean leeks well and boil until barely tender in lightly salted water.
2 Cook finely chopped shallots on low heat in 15–25g ($\frac{1}{2}$–1oz) butter until shiny. Cut ham into small cubes and heat in the butter.
3 Add 1–2 × 5ml tsp (1–2tsp) white wine vinegar, bring to the boil and mix in cream. Season to taste with salt and pepper.
4 Drain leeks well and place in a hot dish. Pour ham sauce on top and sprinkle with finely chopped parsley, or serve parsley separately.

Black Salsify in Cream Sauce – an unusual vegetable dish.

Ratatouille –
Ratatouille à la Niçoise

(serves 4)
Preparation time: 15–20 min
Salting time: 30–45 min
Cooking time: about 40 min
Suitable for the freezer

2 medium-sized aubergines (egg
  plants)
2 onions
1 green pepper
4 tomatoes
1 clove garlic
about 100ml (4fl oz) olive oil
salt, pepper
parsley
basil

1 Wash aubergines and cut into slices or cubes. Leave the skin on unless it is thick or tough. Place in a sieve or colander, sprinkle with coarse salt and place something on top to give light pressure.
2 Peel and coarsely chop onions. Deseed pepper and cut into strips. Scald, peel and quavter tomatoes. Rinse and dry aubergines.
3 Heat olive oil in a saucepan. First sauté onions until golden, then add the other vegetables including crushed garlic. Season with salt and pepper. Add 1 × 15ml tbsp (1tbsp) finely chopped parsley and 2–3 × 15ml tbsp (2–3tbsp) finely chopped fresh, or 1 × 5ml tsp (1tsp) dried, basil.
4 Cover, and simmer until vegetables are very soft. Season to taste with salt and pepper.
Serve hot with all meat dishes. It can also be served cold on toast as a first course, or light evening snack.

Dauphine Potatoes –
Pommes de terre à la
Dauphine

(serves 4)
Preparation time: 15 min
Cooking time: about 30 min
Suitable for the freezer

4–6 large potatoes
50g (2oz) butter
60g (2½oz) plain flour
2 eggs
salt, pepper, nutmeg
2 × 15ml tbsp (2tbsp) grated cheese
oil or lard for frying

1 Boil peeled and sliced potatoes in saltless water. Drain and mash.

Potatoes with Basil –
Pommes de terre au Pistou

(above)
(serves 4)
Preparation time: 10 min
Cooking time: about 15 min
Unsuitable for the freezer

1kg (2¼lb) potatoes
25g (1oz) butter
2 × 15ml tbsp (2tbsp) olive oil
2 onions
2 cloves garlic
salt, black pepper
4–5 × 15ml tbsp (4–5tbsp) basil

1 Peel potatoes and cut into similar-sized pieces. Cook until lightly golden in butter and 1 × 15ml tbsp (1tbsp) oil in a large deep frying pan, and sprinkle with salt and pepper.
2 Peel and coarsely chop onions. Mix with potatoes and fry on low heat until both are tender, turning over from time to time so that the potatoes get an even colour.
3 Mix crushed garlic with remaining oil and chopped basil. Pour over potatoes. Serve hot with fried meat, fish or poultry.

Aubergines with Olives.

2 Bring 100ml (4fl oz) water to the boil with the butter. Sprinkle flour into the water and stir vigorously until mixture boils. Remove from heat, and cool a little.

3 Whisk eggs and stir into the flour mixture, one at a time. Then mix in the mashed potato, grated cheese, nutmeg and salt and pepper to taste.

4 Heat oil or lard to about 180°C (350°F) in a heavy saucepan. Drop in walnut-sized balls of potato. Do not put too many in at a time – one layer is enough – as the balls need space to expand. Fry until golden brown and place on kitchen paper to drain. Serve hot with meat or fish.

Melt-in-the-mouth Potatoes – Pommes de terre Fondantes

(serves 4)
Preparation time: 10 min
Cooking time: 15–25 min
Unsuitable for the freezer

¾–1kg (about 2lb) small potatoes
75g (3oz) butter
sea salt
parsley

1 Peel potatoes and dry in a cloth or kitchen paper.

2 Melt the butter over moderate heat in a large saucepan or casserole. Add potatoes.

3 Cover, and cook potatoes until nearly tender, shaking pan from time to time. Increase heat, remove lid, and shake pan until potatoes are tender and lightly browned. Sprinkle with sea salt and finely chopped parsley.

Aubergines with Olives – Caponata

(serves 4)
Preparation time: 15–20 min
Salting time: 30–45 min
Cooking time: about 30 min
Suitable for the freezer, but will lose some flavour

2 small aubergines
2 green peppers
3 × 15ml tbsp (3tbsp) olive oil
4 ripe tomatoes
salt, pepper
1 stalk of celery
about 100g (¼lb) black olives

2 cloves garlic
1 × 5ml tsp (1tsp) sugar
finely chopped parsley
½–1 × 15ml tbsp (½–1tbsp) wine vinegar

1 Wash aubergines, and peel if the skin is thick and tough. Cut into fairly thick slices, then cut these into two. Sprinkle with salt and place in a sieve with something to give light pressure on top.

2 Wash and deseed peppers. Slice into broad strips. Rinse aubergine slices.

3 Sauté aubergine and peppers in oil in a saucepan on low heat for about 5 min. Remove from pan and place in peeled and quartered tomatoes, sliced celery, olives and crushed garlic. Simmer, covered, for about 15 min and season with salt and pepper. Add wine vinegar and sugar to obtain the right sweet and sour flavour.

4 Return aubergine and paprika mixture to the pan and simmer for 8–10 min. Garnish with parsley and serve cold as a first course, with French bread or toast.

Salads

*In France a 'green salad'
nearly always consists solely
of leaves of various kinds of
lettuce or dandelion, spinach,
nettles etc.
Such a salad is usually served
with a simple dressing
consisting of wine vinegar,
salt, pepper and a vegetable
(eg olive) oil.
More substantial salads are
usually served as either a first
course or after the main
course.*

Mediterranean Salad –
Salade Niçoise
(serves 6)
Preparation time: 15 min
Unsuitable for the freezer

*1 lettuce (only light-coloured heart
   should be used)
4 large tomatoes
1 onion
1 red and 1 green pepper
3 hardboiled eggs
1 × 198g (7oz) can tuna fish in oil
100g (¼lb) black olives
6 anchovy fillets
200g (7oz) cooked green beans
2 × 15ml tbsp (2tbsp) wine vinegar
salt, black pepper
6–8 × 15ml tbsp (6–8tbsp) olive oil
1 clove garlic
basil*

1 Rinse and shred the small lettuce
leaves. Arrange in a salad bowl.
Wash tomatoes and cut into
wedges, slice peeled onion into
paper-thin rings. Wash and deseed
peppers, and cut into thin strips.
2 Slice hardboiled eggs or cut into
wedges. Drain the liquid from the
can of tuna and cut fish meat into
pieces. Finely slice the anchovy fillets, and slice the green beans.
Remove stones from olives.
3 Carefully mix all ingredients in

*Salade Niçoise is truly a French
culinary classic.*

the salad bowl with two forks and
sprinkle over a dressing consisting
of vinegar, salt, coarsely ground
black pepper, oil, crushed garlic
and ½ × 15ml tbsp (½tbsp) fresh, or
½ × 5ml tsp (½tsp) dried, basil.
Serve as a first course with French
bread or toast.

Dandelion Salad –
Salade de Pissenlit
(serves 4)
Preparation time: 5 min
Unsuitable for the freezer

*½–¾ litre (1–1¼pt) young dandelion
   leaves
1 × 15ml tbsp (1tbsp) wine vinegar
½ × 5ml tsp (½tsp) salt
¼ × 5ml tsp (¼tsp) black pepper
4–5 × 15ml tbsp (4–5tbsp) olive oil*

1 Pick the dandelion leaves in an
area you know to be free from any
weedkiller and well away from busy
roads. It is the small light-green
leaves which are used in salads.
2 Rinse leaves several times in cold
water and shake off excess moisture.
3 Mix salt, pepper and vinegar.
Stir or whisk in the oil, and sprinkle
dandelion leaves with the dressing
just before serving.

VARIATION
Fry a few bacon cubes and sprinkle
on top of the salad, or mix dandelion leaves with small cubes of a
mild, firm yellow cheese.

Potato Salad –
Salade de Pommes de terre
(serves 4)
Preparation time: 10 min
Cooking time: 15–20 min
Unsuitable for the freezer

*¾kg (1lb 10oz) firm potatoes
1 × 15ml tbsp (1tbsp) tarragon
   vinegar
salt, pepper, chives
4–5 × 15ml tbsp (4–5tbsp) olive oil*

1 Wash potatoes and boil until
tender without peeling. Pour off
water, cover potatoes with cold
water, and peel.
2 Slice potatoes while still warm,
and sprinkle with a dressing of vinegar, salt, pepper, snipped chives
and oil. Allow salad to settle for a
couple of minutes if you are serving
it warm, turning the potato slices so

that they are evenly covered by the
dressing. For serving cold, place
bowl of potatoes in a cool place for a
couple of hours. Adjust seasoning
before serving.

Bean and Tomato Salad –
Salade de Haricots Verts
et Tomates
(serves 6)
Preparation time: 15 min
Cooking time: about 15 min
Unsuitable for the freezer

*½kg (1lb 2oz) French beans
250g (9oz) tomatoes
French Dressing*

1 Wash beans, slice, and boil in
lightly salted water until tender.
2 Place well-drained and cooled
beans in a salad bowl and carefully
mix in the sliced tomato. Pour
French Dressing over.

French Dressing
French Dressing is simple to make
and frequently used. Oil and vinegar
are mixed as follows:

*3 × 15ml tbsp (3tbsp) oil to 1 × 15ml
   tbsp (1tbsp) wine vinegar
salt and pepper to taste*

Mix ingredients lightly together,
and pour or sprinkle over salad.

Parisian-style Salad –
Salade Parisienne
(serves 4)
Preparation time: 15 min

*Left-overs of cooked meat or ham
3–4 cold boiled potatoes
1 onion
1–2 hardboiled eggs
2–3 tomatoes
1 lettuce
finely chopped parsley
French Dressing*

1 Cut meat into cubes and place in
a large salad bowl with the sliced
potatoes, chopped onion, sliced or
wedge-cut eggs, sliced tomatoes and
shredded lettuce leaves.
2 Mix together 1 quantity of French
Dressing. Pour over the salad and
sprinkle with finely chopped
parsley.
Serve salad as a first course with
toasted French bread or butter-fried
slices of white loaf.

Rabbit and Hare

Rabbit in Mustard Sauce –
Lapin Dijonnaise (right)
(serves 4)
Preparation time: 20 min
Cooking time: 45–60 min
Suitable for the freezer

1 skinned and cleaned rabbit
15g (½oz) butter
1 × 15ml tbsp (1tbsp) oil
salt, pepper
200ml (7fl oz) dry white wine
½–1 × 15ml tbsp (½–1tbsp) Dijon
*   mustard*

200–300ml (7–10fl oz) sour cream
finely chopped parsley

1 Divide the rabbit into neat joints
and dry well. Brown in butter and
oil in a saucepan. Sprinkle with a
little salt and pepper.
2 Blend white wine and mustard
and pour mixture into pot. Turn
meat, cover, and simmer on low heat
until tender.
3 Carefully stir in sour cream.
Bring to the boil and add more mustard and salt if necessary. Sprinkle
with finely chopped parsley.
Serve piping hot with boiled potatoes sprinkled with parsley.

Hare in Red Wine –
Râble de Liévre au Vin Rouge
(centre)
(serves 5–6)
Preparation time: 30 min
Cooking time: about 1 hr
Suitable for the freezer

1 large hare (back and thighs)
25g (1oz) butter
1 × 15ml tbsp (1tbsp) oil
2 onions
juniper berries
salt, pepper
1½ × 15ml tbsp (1½tbsp) plain flour
250ml (9fl oz) beef stock
about 300ml (½pt) rich red wine

52

1 bay leaf
1 sprig of thyme

1 Joint meat, dry well and brown in butter and oil in a saucepan. Add finely chopped onions, salt, coarsely ground black pepper and a few crushed juniper berries.
2 Sprinkle with flour and turn meat until flour is lightly golden and free from lumps. Add stock, red wine, bay leaf and thyme. Simmer, co-vered, on low heat. The back will be tender before the thighs and should be removed first and kept hot.
Serve piping hot with brown bread, boiled potatoes and vegetables.

**Rabbit with Olives –
Lapin aux Olives** (left)
(serves 4–5)
Preparation time: 20 min
Cooking time: 45–60 min
Suitable for the freezer

1 skinned and gutted rabbit
25g (1oz) butter
1 × 15ml tbsp (1tbsp) oil
salt
pepper
2 onions
1 × 15ml tbsp (1tbsp) plain flour
2 bay leaves
300–400ml (½–¾pt) dry white wine
100g (¼lb) green olives

1 Divide rabbit into neat joints. Dry meat, put in a saucepan, and sauté lightly in butter and oil. Sprinkle with very little salt and pepper and add coarsely chopped onions. The olives will also make the dish salty.
2 Sprinkle with flour, turning meat so that flour becomes golden and free from lumps. Add wine and bay leaves. Simmer on low heat for 30–40 min.
3 Add olives and continue to simmer until meat is tender. Serve with French bread, boiled fresh vegetables or cooked lentils or Dandelion Salad (page 51).

Game Birds

In France, the most commonly used game birds are pheasants, wood pigeons and partridges. Here, too, French cuisine has its specialities as these few simple, tasty recipes show.

Roast Partridge – Perdrix au Four

(serves 4)
Preparation time: 30 min
Cooking time: 30–40 min
Oven temperature: 220 and 180°C, 425 and 350°F, Gas 7 and 4
Middle grid in the oven
Suitable for the freezer, but will lose some flavour

2 young, meaty partridges
salt, pepper
butter
about 200g (7oz) thinly sliced fat
200–300ml (7–10fl oz) white wine

1 Pluck and draw partridges. Rub inside and out with salt and pepper and place about 25g (½oz) butter inside each.
2 Tie slices of fat to the breast and thighs with scalded cotton. Place birds, on their side in a greased ovenproof dish, in an oven pre-heated to 220°C, 425°F, Gas 7. Brown partridges at this temperature for about 10 min each side. Lower heat to 180°C, 350°F, Gas 4.
3 Place partridges with breasts facing up, pour in 150ml (¼pt) water and 150ml (¼pt) white wine, and roast until birds are tender. The thigh joints should feel loose and the meat juices, tested by inserting a thin needle into the thickest part of thigh, should be light in colour.
4 Remove fat slices, cut partridges into pieces and place on a hot dish. Deglaze ovenproof dish with the remaining white wine and 15–25g (½–1oz) butter, and pour over meat.

Wood Pigeons in Red Wine – Pigeons au Vin Rouge

(serves 4)
Preparation time: 30 min
Cooking time: about ½–1½ hr depending on bird's age
Suitable for the freezer but will lose some flavour

2–4 wood pigeons
50–75g (2–3oz) butter
salt, pepper
2 × 15ml tbsp (2tbsp) brandy (optional)
8–10 shallots
350–400ml (12–15fl oz) dry red wine
250g (9oz) mushrooms
lemon juice

1 Pluck and draw birds. Rub inside and out with salt and pepper. Sauté in 25–40g (1–1½oz) butter in a heavy saucepan or casserole.
2 If you wish to flambé the pigeons, pour over brandy at room temperature and set alight. Shake pan until flames are extinguished.
3 Add peeled shallots to pan, pour over red wine and lower heat a little. Simmer in casserole with a tight-fitting lid, until pigeons are tender. Young birds need 20–30 min, older ones anything up to 1–1½ hr. When tested with a thin needle, the juices from thigh should be light in colour.
4 Sauté whole mushrooms in 15–25g (1–2oz) butter on strong heat. Sprinkle with 1 × 15ml tbsp (1tbsp) lemon juice and season with salt.
Arrange pigeons whole or sliced on a warm dish, together with shallots and mushrooms. Serve with red wine juices, bread and boiled vegetables.

Stuffed Pheasant with Brussels Sprouts – Faisan Farci aux Choux de Bruxelles (right)

(serves 4)
Preparation time: 30 min
Cooking time: ¾–1½ hr
Suitable for the freezer, but will lose some flavour

1 large pheasant
300g (11oz) piece of fat
½kg (1lb 2oz) loin of pork
salt, pepper
nutmeg
1 egg
1 × 15ml tbsp (1tbsp) finely chopped parsley
3 × 15ml tbsp (3tbsp) brandy (optional)
25g (1oz) butter
1 × 15ml tbsp (1tbsp) oil
200ml (7fl oz) stock
300ml (½pt) dry white wine
½kg (1lb 2oz) Brussels sprouts

1 Pluck and draw pheasant. Put liver, gizzard and heart through a mincer with the pork and about 150g (5oz) fat. Mix in 1 × 5ml tsp (1tsp) salt, ¼ × 5ml tsp (¼tsp) nutmeg, egg, parsley and 1 × 15ml tbsp (1tbsp) brandy. If the mince seems too loose, add 1–2 × 15ml tbsp

(1–2tbsp) breadcrumbs.

2 Stuff pheasant. Rub outside of the bird with salt and pepper and tie on slices of fat. Brown nicely on all sides in 15g (½oz) butter and 1 × 15ml tbsp (1tbsp) oil in a heavy saucepan or casserole.

3 Flambé pheasant if wished with 2 × 15ml tbsp (2tbsp) brandy at room temperature. Shake pan until the flames die down.

4 Add stock and wine and simmer pheasant until tender. A young bird takes 20–30 min, an older one anything up to 1½ hr. The thigh joints should feel loose, and the meat juices from thigh or breast should be light in colour when tested with a thin needle.

5 Clean sprouts, boil until nearly tender in lightly salted water. Drain, and sauté in remaining butter. Arrange pheasant and sprouts in a hot dish.

Soufflé au Grand Marnier

1 Use 5 medium-sized eggs. It is important that the eggs are not too cold.

2 Make a mixture of butter, flour and milk. Remove saucepan from heat, whisk egg yolks, and stir them in.

3 Season soufflé with salt, sugar and Grand Marnier. Beat egg whites until soft peaks form – they should not be too dry.

4 Fold in stiffly whisked egg whites as carefully as possible to retain a light texture. Spoon mixture into a soufflé dish and bake at once.

Fluffy Soufflés

Making a delicious soufflé is an art – but an art which is easy to learn.

Liqueur Soufflé –
Soufflé au Grand Marnier
(serves 4)
Preparation time: 20 min
Cooking time: 30–40 min
Oven temperature: 180–190°C, 350–375°F, Gas 4–5
Bottom part of the oven
Unsuitable for the freezer

25g (1oz) butter
3 × 15ml tbsp (3tbsp) flour
250ml (9fl oz) milk
salt
3 × 15ml tbsp (3tbsp) sugar
5 eggs, separated
3–4 × 15ml tbsp (3–4tbsp) Grand Marnier
butter and breadcrumbs for dish

1 Melt butter, add flour and beat well together. Gradually add warm milk to form a smooth mixture and simmer for a few minutes. Cool a little.
2 Beat egg yolks and stir into mixture. Add a pinch of salt, sugar and Grand Marnier.
3 Grease and sprinkle a 1 litre (1¾pt) soufflé dish with breadcrumbs. Beat egg whites until soft peaks form. Stir 2–3 × 15ml tbsp 2–3 tbsp of egg white into butter mixture, then carefully fold in the remainder.
4 Pour soufflé mixture into an ovenproof dish and immediately place in oven. Bake as directed for 30–40 min. Serve immediately with apricot purée, flavoured with a little Grand Marnier.

VARIATIONS
Vanilla Soufflé
Bruise a vanilla pod and bring to the boil with the milk. Remove vanilla pod before using milk in recipe. To add extra flavour, add ½–1 × 5ml tsp (½–1tsp) vanilla sugar. Add 1–2 × 15ml tbsp (1–2 tbsp) sweet sherry instead of Grand Marnier.

Mocha Soufflé
Replace Grand Marnier with 2 × 5ml tsp (2tsp) cocoa, 1 × 5ml tsp (1tsp) instant coffee, 3 × 15ml tbsp (3tbsp) strong, cold coffee and 1 × 15ml tbsp (1tbsp) brandy. Add before folding in egg whites.

Prune Soufflé –
Soufflé aux Pruneaux
(serves 4)
Preparation time: 15 min
Steeping time: 12 hr
Baking time: about 30 min
Oven temperature: 220°C, 425°F, Gas 7
Unsuitable for the freezer

300g (11oz) prunes
3 eggs, separated
100g (¼lb) sugar
½ litre (about 1pt) milk
50g (2oz) ground almonds

1 Steep prunes in water overnight, then boil for a few minutes in a little water and 2 × 15ml tbsp (2tbsp) sugar. Remove stones and place in a greased ovenproof dish.
2 Beat remaining sugar and egg yolks well together and stir in warm milk and ground almonds. Whisk egg whites until peaks form, and fold carefully into mixture. Spoon over prunes and bake as directed.

VARIATIONS
Apricot Soufflé –
Soufflé aux Abricots
Replace prunes with 200g (7oz) dried apricots. Steep and boil apricots and make soufflé using the

same method as for Prune Soufflé. You can also use canned apricots. Drain before putting them in the soufflé dish.

Apple Soufflé –
Soufflé aux Pommes
Peel and core 2–3 apples, and cut into wedges. Boil for 2 min in lightly sugared water, add cinnamon to taste. Otherwise follow the method for Prune Soufflé.

Cheese Soufflé –
Soufflé au Fromage
(serves 4)
Preparation time: 20 min
Cooking time: about 30 min
Oven temperature: 180–190°C, 350–375°F, Gas 4–5
Bottom part of the oven
Unsuitable for the freezer

25g (1oz) butter
2 × 15ml tbsp (2tbsp) flour
250ml (9fl oz) milk
½ × 5ml tsp (½tsp) salt
2 × 15ml tbsp (2tbsp) grated
  Parmesan cheese
4–5 × 15ml tbsp (4–5tbsp) grated
  Gruyère cheese
4 eggs, separated
pepper
cayenne
butter and breadcrumbs for dish

1 Melt butter, add flour and simmer for 2 min without allowing it to brown. Gradually stir in warm milk until mixture is smooth. Simmer for 6–8 min. Remove saucepan from heat.
2 Stir in grated cheeses and the lightly whisked egg yolks. Season with salt, freshly ground pepper and

a pinch of cayenne.
3 Grease soufflé dish with 1 × 15ml tbsp (1tbsp) melted butter and sprinkle with breadcrumbs. Beat egg whites until stiff, but not dry. Stir 2–3 × 15ml tbsp (2–3tbsp) egg white into mixture, then carefully fold in the remainder.
4 Spoon mixture into soufflé dish and place on the bottom grid of the oven. Bake as directed for 30 min. Serve immediately with white bread and butter.
NOTE
A soufflé tends to sink a little when you take it out of the oven. To avoid this add ½ × 5ml tsp (½tsp) baking powder, either with, or after you have added, egg yolks. This is not one of the classic rules for making a soufflé, but it works and nobody can tell the difference.

French Tarts with Eggs and Cheese

Serve small or large tarts – containing egg, cheese, cream, ham, onion and various other flavourings – as a lunch dish, part of the dinner, or as informal get-together fare with a glass of beer or wine.

**Small Cheese Tarts –
Tartelettes au Fromage**
(serves 6–8)
Preparation time: 20 min
Cooking time: about 30 min
Oven temperature: 200°C, 400°F, Gas 6
Middle grid of the oven
Unbaked, is suitable for the freezer

*Pastry : 150g (5oz) flour
100g ($\frac{1}{4}$lb) butter
$\frac{1}{2}$ × 5ml tsp ($\frac{1}{2}$tsp) salt
$\frac{1}{2}$ whisked egg
Filling :
100g ($\frac{1}{4}$lb) cottage cheese
50g (2oz) butter
$\frac{1}{2}$ × 15ml tbsp ($\frac{1}{2}$tbsp) flour
1$\frac{1}{2}$ whisked eggs
50g (2oz) firm, grated cheese
1 × 15ml tbsp (1tbsp) chopped
    parsley*

1 Rub butter into flour with the fingertips. Add salt and mix to a dough with $\frac{1}{2}$ whisked egg. Leave in a cool place for 20–30 min.
2 For filling, mix cottage cheese with softened butter. Stir in flour and whisked eggs to form a smooth mixture. Add grated cheese and chopped parsley.
3 Roll out pastry and line small individual tins. Divide cheese mixture between them and bake as directed.
Serve warm with a green salad.

*Above left : Small Cheese Tarts for the special guest.
Left : Ham Tart is just the thing when you want to serve something simple.*

**Ham Tart –
Tarte au Jambon**
(serves 4–6)
Preparation time: 30 min
Cooking time: about 30 min
Oven temperature: 200°C, 400°F,
Gas 6
Middle grid in the oven
Filled but unbaked, is suitable for
the freezer

*1 quantity pastry as for Small
    Cheese Tarts*
Filling:
4 large onions
25g (1oz) butter
2 hardboiled eggs
150g (5oz) cooked ham
3 egg yolks
25ml (9fl oz) double cream
100g (¼lb) cream cheese
salt, pepper
chives

1 Leave dough in a cool place for a
while. Meanwhile prepare filling.
2 Peel onions, and slice into thin

rings. Sauté in the butter on low
heat until soft and transparent.
Remove frying pan or saucepan
from heat.
3 Coarsely chop the hardboiled
eggs. Cut ham into cubes and add
both to the onion. Beat egg yolks
with cream and mashed cream
cheese, and add to the onion mixture. Season with salt, pepper and
finely chopped chives.
4 Roll out pastry and line an ovenproof dish, about 22cm (8½in) in
diameter, spoon in filling and bake.

**Bacon and Egg Tart –
La Quiche Lorraine**
(serves 4)
Preparation time: 20 min
Oven temperature: 240 and 200°C,
475 and 400°F, Gas 9 and 6
Cooking time: 25–30 min
Middle part of the oven
Filled and unbaked is suitable for
the freezer

La Quiche Lorraine is always a success – simple to make, yet full of flavour.

*1 quantity pastry as for Small
    Cheese Tarts*
Filling:
125g (4½oz) bacon
3 eggs
300ml (½pt) single cream
100g (¼lb) grated Gruyère cheese
pepper, salt
paprika

1 Cool dough for a while, then roll
out to line a greased flan tin about
22cm (8½in) in diameter. Prick base
and bake blind for about 8 min at
240°C, 475°F, Gas 9.
2 Cut bacon into thin strips and
sauté lightly in a frying pan. Place in
semi-baked tart shell. Beat eggs with
cream and grated cheese. Season
with pepper, paprika and a pinch of
salt.
3 Pour egg mixture over bacon
strips, place tin in oven, and bake
tart at 200°C, 400°F, Gas 6 for
15–20 min.

Omelettes

It's not at all difficult to make a real French omelette if you make it with care, speed, freshly laid eggs and – last but not least – a good frying pan!

The omelette pan should be made of iron or aluminium, with sloping sides. Frying pans with a non-stick coating are excellent too. An ordinary frying pan, unless it has been scrubbed often with scouring powder, will make perfect omelettes.

French Omelette
(basic recipe)
Omelette Naturelle
(serves 2–3)
Preparation time: 5 min
Cooking time: about 3 min
Unsuitable for the freezer

4 eggs
15g (½oz) butter
½ × 5ml tsp (½tsp) salt
pinch of white pepper

1 Heat frying pan. Beat eggs lightly with salt and pepper.
2 Heat butter in frying pan until it has stopped sizzling and pour in egg mixture. Increase heat a little.
3 Move a fork to and fro along the bottom of the pan a couple of times, while shaking the pan slightly. The egg mixture will then set smoothly.
4 The omelette is ready when it has set along the bottom and edge of the pan but is still slightly moist on top.

Basque Omelette is served straight from the pan with bread and a couple of slices of ham.

Tilt omelette towards the handle, while tapping same. The omelette will then fold over. Slide carefully onto a hot serving dish and serve.

This is the basic recipe for the creamy French omelette. The following recipes are variations with different kinds of filling. Remember always to have the filling ready and kept warm. Place either in or on omelette mixture, at start or when it is half cooked.

Spinach Omelette –
Omelette aux Épinards
(serves 2–3)
Preparation time: 15 min
Cooking time: about 10 min
Unsuitable for the freezer

300g (11oz) spinach
1 shallot
25g (1oz) butter
salt, pepper
nutmeg
4 eggs

1 Rinse spinach several times in cold water and cut off the roughest stalks. Sauté finely chopped shallot and spinach in 15g (½oz) butter for 5–6 min. Season with salt, pepper and grated nutmeg.
2 Beat eggs lightly with salt and pepper and fry omelette until nearly done in remaining butter (see French Omelette).
3 Place spinach mixture on egg mixture and finish cooking omelette.

Basque Omelette –
La Pipérade
(serves 2–3)
Preparation time: 15 min
Salting time: 30–45 min
Cooking time: about 20 min
Unsuitable for the freezer

1 small aubergine (egg plant)
salt
1 onion
1 clove garlic
2 × 15ml tbsp (2tbsp) olive oil
1 green pepper
1 × 10cm (4in) piece of cucumber
  OR 1 courgette
4 tomatoes
1 × 15ml tbsp (1tbsp) chopped parsley
1 × 15ml tbsp (1tbsp) fresh or ½ × 5ml tsp (½tsp) dried basil
4 eggs, white pepper

1 Wash aubergine, slice and place slices in a colander or sieve. Sprinkle with a pinch of salt and put under slight pressure.

2 Sauté chopped onion and crushed garlic in the oil for 5 min. Add deseeded sliced pepper, rinsed aubergine slices, cucumber slices and quartered tomatoes. Sauté vegetables for about 10 min, then sprinkle with salt, pepper, finely chopped parsley and fresh or dried basil.

3 Beat eggs lightly with salt and pepper and fry omelette until nearly ready in an omelette pan (see French Omelette).

4 Place vegetable mixture on top of omelette and finish cooking. The egg mixture can also be poured over the vegetables and fried until omelette is firm at the bottom and creamy on top. Serve with French bread and cooked ham.

**Mushroom Omelette –
Omelette Forestière**
(serves 2–3)
Preparation time: 15 min
Cooking time: about 10 min
Unsuitable for the freezer

2 shallots
1 clove garlic
150–200g (5–7oz) mushrooms
salt, pepper
4 eggs
butter
lemon juice
parsley

Above: Spinach Omelette.
Left: Mushroom Omelette.

1 Sauté finely chopped shallots and crushed garlic in 15g ($\frac{1}{2}$oz) butter for 3–4 min. Add cleaned or peeled sliced mushrooms and continue to sauté the lot on strong heat. Add $\frac{1}{2} \times 5$ml tsp ($\frac{1}{2}$tsp) salt and 1×15ml tbsp (1tbsp) lemon juice and turn off heat.

2 Beat eggs lightly with salt and pepper and bake omelette until nearly done (see French Omelette).

3 Spoon the warm mushrooms over the egg mixture and finish cooking omelette. Serve immediately with ham or smoked pork and garnished with parsley.

Delicious Sweets

Apple Cake –
Gâteau aux Pommes (above left)
(serves 4–6)
Preparation time: 20 min
Cooking time: about 45 min
Oven temperature: 190–200°C,
375–400°F, Gas 5–6

5–6 apples, ½ lemon
75g (3oz) sugar, ½ vanilla pod
100g (¼lb) raisins
1 × 15ml tbsp (1tbsp) rum
200g (7oz) cottage cheese
2 eggs, separated
4 × 15ml tbsp (4tbsp) cornflour
½ × 5ml tsp (½tsp) baking powder
1 × 5ml tsp (1tsp) cinnamon
25–40g (1–1½oz) butter

1 Peel and core apples and cut into
wedges. Sprinkle with lemon juice
and place in a greased ovenproof
dish. Sprinkle 50g (2oz) sugar over
and finely chopped vanilla pod.
2 Place raisins in rum and leave to
settle for 2–3 min. Mix cottage
cheese with egg yolks and cornflour
mixed with baking powder. Carefully stir in raisins and stiffly
whisked egg whites.
3 Spread mixture evenly over

apples, sprinkle with remaining
sugar and the cinnamon, and place a
few dollops of butter on the top.
Bake as directed and serve warm.

Pancakes with Walnuts –
Crêpes aux Noix (above right)
(serves 4)
Preparation time: 10 min
Cooking time: about 15 min

2 eggs, 60g (2½oz) flour
2 × 15ml tbsp (2tbsp) sugar
50g (2oz) butter
100ml (4fl oz) single cream
100g (¼lb) raisins
2 × 15ml tbsp (2tbsp) rum
4–5 × 15ml tbsp (4–5tbsp) honey
25–50g (1–2oz) walnuts
butter for frying

1 Combine eggs, flour, sugar,
melted butter, cream and ½ × 15ml
tbsp (½tbsp) rum to make a smooth
batter. Place raisins in remaining
rum.
2 Fry thin pancakes in a little butter
and fold into 2 or 4.
3 Heat honey over low heat. Turn
one pancake at a time in the liquid
honey and place about 1 × 15ml tbsp
(1tbsp) rum and raisin mixture, and
walnuts, on top, or as illustration.

Pear Tart –
Tourte aux Poires (left)
(serves 4–6)
Preparation time: 20 min
Cooking time: about 30 min
Oven temperature: 200°C, 400°F,
Gas 6

Pastry: 250g (9oz) flour
150g (5oz) butter, 50g (2oz) sugar
1 egg, 1 egg for brushing
Filling: ¾kg (1lb 10oz) pears
100g (¼lb) sugar
½ × 5ml tsp (½tsp) cinnamon
100ml (4fl oz) double cream

1 Rub butter into flour with the
fingertips, add sugar and mix until
smooth with 1 lightly beaten egg.
Leave in a cool place for 20 min.
2 Roll out dough and use two-thirds
to line base and sides of a greased
ovenproof dish. Prick base well with
a fork, place tinfoil along the sides
and fill with dried peas etc.
3 Bake for 12–15 min, then remove
from oven. Take out peas and foil.
Place in peeled and sliced pears,
sprinkle with sugar and a little cinnamon. Pour cream over and fit a
pastry top. Squeeze edges tightly
together, brush with beaten egg and
make a hole in lid. Bake as directed.

Index